CROCHET AMIGURUMI

FOR EVERY OCCASION

THE WOoBLES

CROCHET AMIGURUMI

FOR EVERY OCCASION

21 Easy Projects to Celebrate Life's Happy Moments

JUSTINE TIU

weldon**owen**

SAN RAFAEL · LOS ANGELES · LONDON

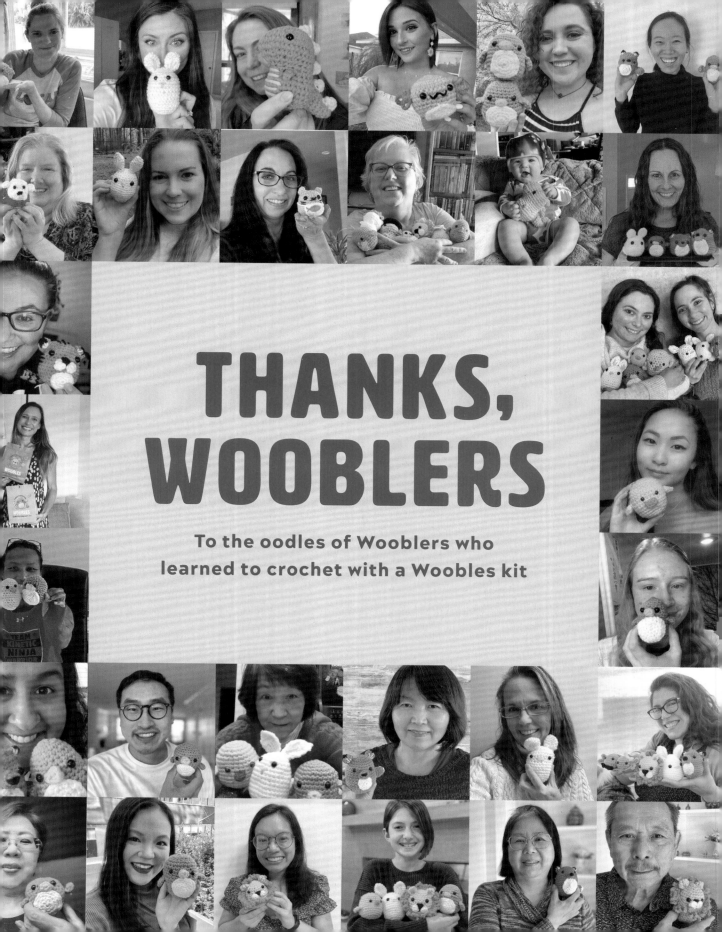

THANKS, WOOBLERS

To the oodles of Wooblers who
learned to crochet with a Woobles kit

CONTENTS

INTRODUCTION

I'm Justine, co-founder of The Woobles. We made the first crochet kit that taught tens of thousands of complete beginners (and counting!) to crochet.

I went down the rabbit hole of amigurumi—the art of crocheting small, stuffed yarn plushies—back in 2016, when I wanted to make a personalized gift for a friend. What could be more personal than a handmade plushie of her favorite animal?

So off I went, piecing together YouTube videos, diagrams, and crochet blogs. I rejiggered what I found to fit what I was working on. I made a lot of mistakes, and I did a lot more of hoping for the best.

In the end, I made a very lumpy and misshapen penguin (pictured to the left). Lumpy and mis-shapen as he was, I was still proud of him. My friend adored him. And to my delight, so did everyone else who caught a glimpse of him too.

And that, my woobly friend, is why I made this book – so that you can experience and share that joy, too.

If it's your first time crocheting, start learning the basics with a Woobles beginner kit from **thewoobles.com/kits**. If you're already comfy with grabbing yarn with a hook and putting the hook in the right hole (yep, that's crocheting in a nutshell), then you're ready to tackle any pattern in this book.

One more thing before you get wooblin'. You'll notice that the patterns get more elaborate toward the end of each section. Some of the patterns might look a bit beyond what you think you can do right now, but don't worry—that's what The Woobles is all about: proving to yourself that you can always learn something new. You'd be surprised by how much you can learn, a little bit at a time.

So get ready. You're about to blow your friends' and family's minds with the most heartfelt hand-made crocheted gifts. Better yet, you're going to do it **without** the frustration of piecing together YouTube videos, diagrams, and crochet blogs while hoping for the best. (I can make no guaran-tees on the mistakes part, though. When it comes to crochet, that's just a part of the journey.)

Everything you need to know to make any pat-tern in this book is either in the book or on our website. Because as nice as it is to do something completely offline, sometimes you just need a good new-fashioned video to make things click.

I hope this book becomes your go-to resource to make the cutest crochet memories for many years to come. I hope the amigurumi you make from this book instantly bring huge smiles to you and your loved ones' faces. And I hope the skills you learn from this book give you the confidence to keep pushing yourself to try new things.

Happy wooblin'!

Justine

EVERYTHING YOU NEED

When it comes down to it, you only need two things to crochet: yarn and a crochet hook.

YARN

All the projects in this book use The Woobles Easy Peasy Yarn. If you're pretty new to crocheting, I recommend using this yarn because it's been custom-made for beginners. It's more like a drawstring and less like what you might traditionally think of as yarn, which means two great things for beginners:

1. **It can't split.** Say goodbye to snagged hooks and frayed yarn.

2. **It's easy to see your stitches.** No more second-guessing if you're looking at a stitch, or just some pesky yarn fibers that make up the stitch.

Your final amigurumi will come out looking a lot cleaner, too! If you can't get your hands on The Woobles Easy Peasy Yarn, you can use any medium-weight #4 yarn.

YARN WEIGHT

Yarn weight sounds like it refers to, well, weight. But surprise! It doesn't; it actually refers to thickness. The higher the number, the fatter the yarn. There are eight weights, which usually look something like this on a yarn label.

Multiple types of yarn fall into each weight category:

WEIGHT	CATEGORY	TYPES
0	Lace	Fingering
1	Super Fine	Sock, Fingering, Baby
2	Fine	Sport, Baby
3	Light	DK, Light Worsted
4	Medium	Worsted, Afghan, Aran
5	Bulky	Chunky, Craft, Rug
6	Super Bulky	Super Bulky, Roving
7	Jumbo	Jumbo, Roving

Patterns might reference the category or type of yarn. If you ever want to swap out a pattern's recommended yarn but still want your piece to come out the same size, pick a yarn in the same weight category.

HOOKS

Crochet hooks come in lots of materials and sizes. The most common materials are plastic, aluminum, and bamboo. Each one has its pros and cons when it comes to cost, ergonomics, and ease of gliding yarn on the hook.

I personally like hooks with an aluminum shaft and rubber handle. Yarn glides smooth like butter on an aluminum shaft, and the size and feel of a rubber handle make it easy to hold.

As for hook size, that's determined by yarn weight–which, remember, really means yarn thickness. The thicker the yarn, the bigger the hook you'll need. Luckily, patterns take the guesswork out by recommending both a yarn weight and hook size.

Hook sizes can be written in letters or millimeters. Different companies define letters differently, so just to be safe, I recommend choosing hooks based on millimeters. The millimeters refer to the diameter of the hook, and math don't lie. Here are some common hook sizes:

MILLIMETER	US SIZE	UK SIZE
2.25	B-1	13
2.75	C-2	11
3.25	D-3	10
3.5	E-4	-
3.75	F-5	9
4	G-6	8
4.5	-	7
5	H-8	6
5.5	I-9	5
6	J-10	4

If you're picking your own yarn, the yarn label will have a recommended hook size that looks something like this: in this case, an I-9 / 5.5mm hook. ⟶ [5.5 mm / I-9]

TIP When crocheting amigurumi, use a slightly smaller hook than what's recommended on the label. This way, your stitches will be smaller and it's less likely the stuffing will show. I tend to size down by at least 1mm.

All the patterns in this book use a US G-6 / 4mm hook.

TIP Since everyone crochets slightly differently, you might want to play with the size of the hook to get the ideal stitch size. For example, if you notice lots of holes in your amigurumi, go half a millimeter down in hook size. If it's hard to put the hook under a stitch, go half a millimeter up in hook size.

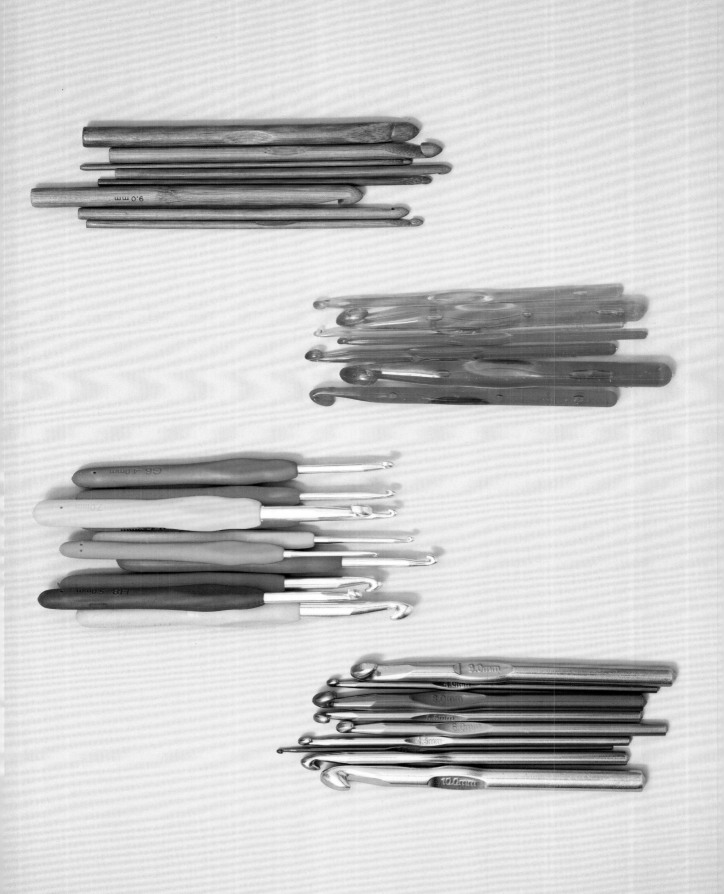

OTHER EQUIPMENT

There are a few other items that'll help you out as you start making amigurumi.

1. Stuffing

Amigurumi is filled with stuffing, which is usually made from polyester or cotton. You can also repurpose filling from old cushions and pillows.

2. Scissors

While I wish we could crochet forever, at some point, you'll need to separate your yarn from the rest of the yarn ball. To get a clean cut of The Woobles Easy Peasy Yarn, use sharp scissors. The sharper, the better.

TIP Don't have scissors? Use nail clippers instead.

3. Safety eyes

Safety eyes help give some character and life to your amigurumi. They come in lots of shapes, sizes, and colors. They're great for handmade plushies because they're easy to attach and difficult to remove.

Safety eyes are measured by diameter in millimeters. All but one of the patterns in this book use black 10mm eyes. One pattern, Sugar and Snow the Two Peas in a Pod (pages 77-81), uses black 8mm eyes.

TIP Safety eyes are ironically not safe for small children or pets. You can always embroider eyes instead (see tutorial on page 56).

4. Tapestry needle

Also called a yarn needle or darning needle, a tapestry needle has a really big eye and a blunt tip. It can be made of metal or plastic. You'll thread this needle with your yarn tails to finish any crocheted piece.

5. Stitch markers

Because amigurumi is crocheted in continuous rounds (see tutorial on page 20), you won't be able to tell where a round begins and ends. This matters because you need to keep count of how many stitches you've made in each round, otherwise you might end up with a doily instead of a penguin. So, what's a Woobler to do? Use stitch markers.

There are a few different styles of stitch markers. My favorites are the ones that look like safety pins, because it's impossible for them to fall off. Learn how to use them properly on page 24.

6. Sewing pins

When it's time to sew together the different parts of your amigurumi, it can be helpful to have sewing pins to help keep the wee woobly pieces in place.

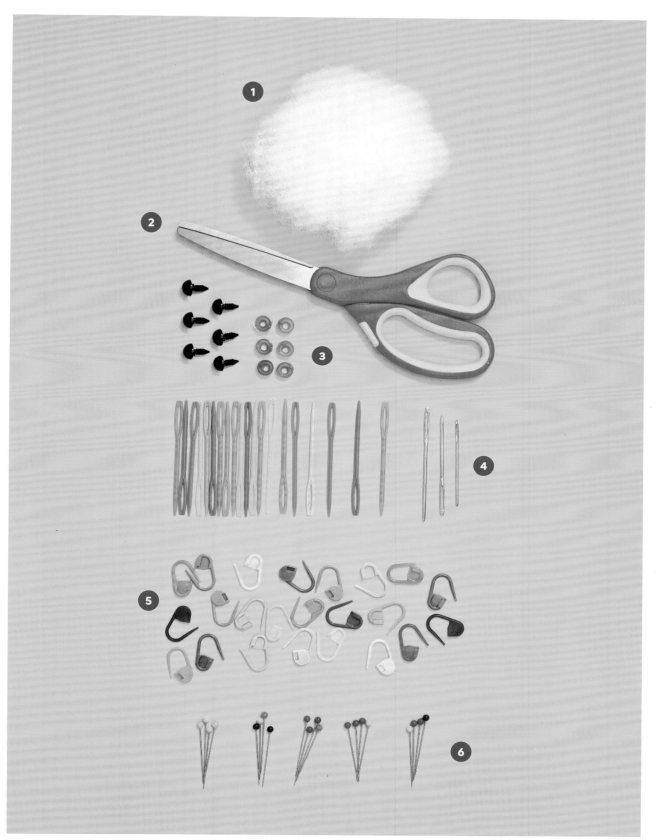

EVERYTHING YOU NEED TO KNOW

Think of this section as a quick reference guide to be able to follow any pattern in this book. It's organized into three parts: the Basics, Stitches, and Techniques. Each part is ordered by what you need to know first, either in terms of complexity or when you'd use it in a pattern.

If it's your first time crocheting, I highly recommend learning the basics with a Woobles beginner kit. It'll guide you through the whole process of

crocheting your first amigurumi, so that you'll be more ready to take on both the ultra-beginner and slightly more advanced patterns in this book.

All the photos and tutorials in this book are for righties. Left-handed? Hold the book up to a mirror to see what it looks like to swap the hook and yarn hands. That's much easier said than done, so for the best experience, go to **thewoobles.com** for left-handed photo and video tutorials.

It can be tricky to learn from just photos, which is why we also have both right- and left-handed video tutorials for everything at **thewoobles.com/tutorials**.

BASICS

▶ Follow right- and left-handed video tutorials at **thewoobles.com/tutorials**

How to hold a hook

Hold the hook with your right hand. There are two ways to hold a crochet hook. Do what's comfiest for you:

1. Hold the hook like a knife.

2. Or hold the hook like a pencil, resting the hook on your middle finger and holding it between your thumb and pointer finger.

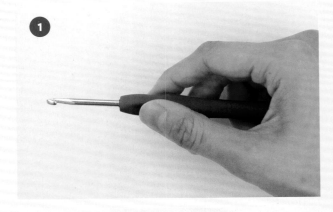

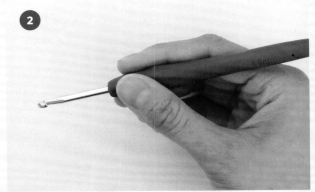

How to hold yarn

Hold the yarn with your left hand. There are lots of ways to hold yarn—the way I hold it is the way my mom taught me. Just like with the hook grip, do what's comfiest for you. The most important thing is to keep constant tension with the working yarn, so that your stitches come out evenly.

Did you read that last sentence and wonder—does my yarn have a 9-to-5 job? Let's pause and cover some terminology:

WORKING YARN: the yarn connected to the ball. It's the yarn you'll literally "work" with to crochet.

TAIL: the end of the yarn

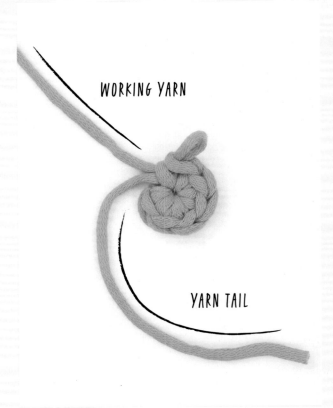

WORKING YARN

YARN TAIL

How to hold yarn (continued)

1. Turn your left palm to face you. Hold your piece in front of your hand.

2. Wrap the working yarn once around your pinky, so that the piece ends up behind your hand.

3. Bring the piece up the back of your hand until you can drape it over your pointer finger.

4. Hold onto the piece with your thumb and middle finger. Move the yarn tail behind your piece. To tighten or loosen the tension of the working yarn, move your pointer finger toward or away from you. The loop for the hook should be in the upper right-hand corner, and your next stitch will be crocheted to the left.

TIP If your working yarn is super loose after following these steps, try doing step 2 as close as possible to your piece.

When you put it all together, the hook should be in front of your working yarn. Your final crocheting position should look something like this:

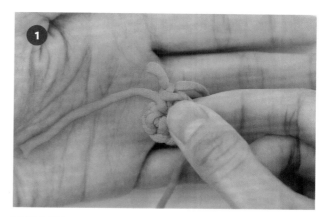

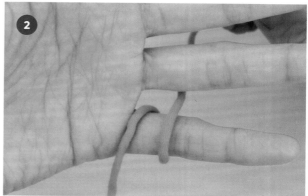

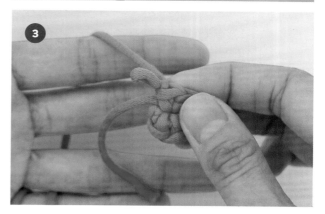

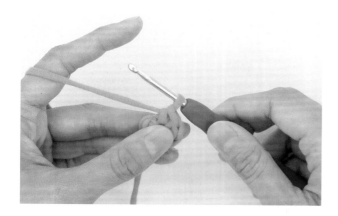

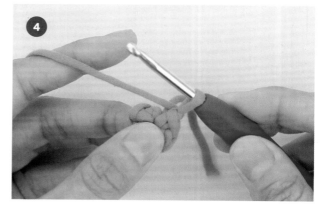

Count stitches, rows, and rounds

When you crochet, you make what are called "stitches." The top loops of a stitch, which is where you usually put your crochet hook, look like a horizontal V:

From the side, a stitch looks like a vertical V:

Stitches can be worked in rows (like a blanket), or rounds (like a hat or plushie). To crochet the next row or round, crochet into the stitches of the previous row or round.

TIP If you're right-handed, always crochet in the stitches to the left. If you're left-handed, always crochet in the stitches to the right.

TIP When counting stitches in a row or round, do not count the loop on the hook as a stitch.

The number and types of stitches in each row or round determine what the final crochet piece looks like.

A row is a horizontal line of stitches. Row 6 is made of 10 stitches:

A round is a complete circle of stitches. Round 2 is made of 12 stitches:

Rounds can either be crocheted as "joined rounds" or "continuous rounds." The difference is in the transition from one round to the next.

Joined rounds have a clear beginning and end. The end of one round is connected to the beginning of the same round with a "join," like a slip stitch and chain. The result is a piece with straight rounds but also a seam.

Most amigurumi, including all the ones in this book, are crocheted in continuous rounds, which means there's no clear beginning and end. The end of one round is immediately followed by the first stitch of the next round. The result is a piece that spirals and has no seam.

Here's a picture of the same pattern, crocheted in joined rounds (left) versus continuous rounds (right). You can see the seam in the left piece:

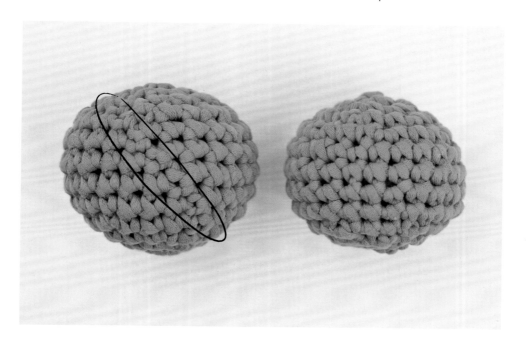

Right vs. wrong side of crochet

There's a so-called right and wrong side of crochet. That sounds a bit harsh, so another way of thinking about it is that there's a front and back side to your work.

Here's a picture of the same pattern, with the wrong side versus the right side facing out. The wrong side has horizontal bars throughout the piece (left). The right side looks like a bunch of Vs (right).

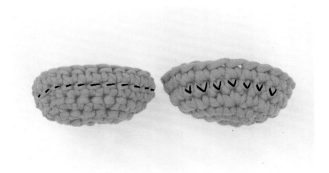

When crocheting in a round, your piece will naturally curl at some point. The direction it naturally curls will make the wrong side face you. To make the right side face you, follow these steps:

1. Make sure the wrong side is facing you. The wrong side has horizontal bars.

2. Push the middle of the piece until it flips inside out.

3. The right side will now be facing you, but your piece will be upside down. To make it easier to keep crocheting . . .

4. Rotate your piece until the open edge is on top of the piece, and the loop for the hook is on the side of the circle closest to you. The outside of your piece should now look like it's made of vertical Vs.

TIP Since it's something that's easy to forget to do, plus patterns don't cue it, get in the habit of flipping your work as soon as possible to make the right side face out.

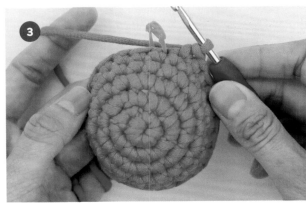

Parts of a crochet stitch

When you're new to crocheting, you'll probably ask yourself: "where, oh where does my crochet hook go next?" after almost every stitch you make.

Unless a pattern says otherwise, put the hook under both legs of the top loop.

Sometimes a pattern might tell you to put the hook through the front loop only (flo) or back loop only (blo). To do that, first make sure the "right side" of your piece is facing you. Then insert the hook under only one leg of the top loop. The leg closer to you is the front loop, and the leg further from you is the back loop.

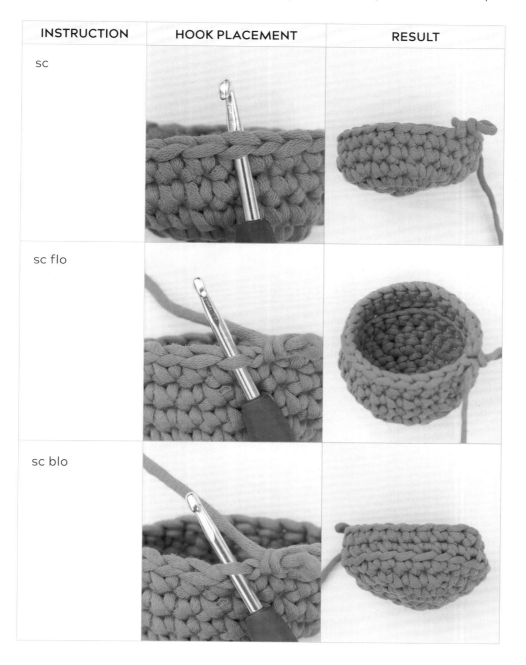

INSTRUCTION	HOOK PLACEMENT	RESULT
sc		
sc flo		
sc blo		

Use stitch markers

Always put a stitch marker under the top loops of the first stitch of your current round. Future you will be oh-so-grateful for a number of reasons:

- You'll catch mistakes early on. Every time you finish a round, count the number of stitches in the round and make sure it matches the pattern. Use the stitch marker as the starting point for the count.

- When you lose count of your stitches, just start counting from the stitch marker to find your place again.

- When you inevitably make a mistake, undo your stitches up to the stitch marked by the stitch marker. (Otherwise, you'll have to undo everything every time you make a mistake. And trust me, that's no fun.)

So do future you a huge favor, and learn how to use stitch markers to properly keep track of your stitches:

1. Crochet the first stitch of the round.

2. Insert the stitch marker under both top loops of the stitch you just made, and clip it closed like a safety pin.

TIP Insert the stitch marker from the front to the back of the piece, with the open edge on the bottom. This way, you can use your thumb to help push the stitch marker open.

3. Crochet the rest of the round as you normally would. When you've crocheted into the last hole before the stitch marker, you're done. Count the number of stitches in the round, starting with the one marked by the stitch marker. (Remember, the loop on the hook does **not** count as a stitch.) If it matches the pattern, then congrats! You can move on to the next round.

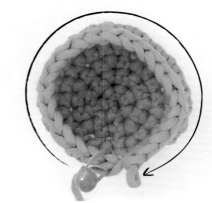

Abbreviations

At first glance, crochet patterns look like a foreign language. They use a lot of abbreviations and symbols, but once you get used to decoding them, they actually make it easier to read a pattern.

Before diving into a pattern, check to see if it's written in US or UK terminology. The same stitches are named differently based on the country. All the patterns in this book are written in US terminology. Here's a list of all the abbreviations used in this book, plus their UK equivalent:

US ABBREVIATIONS	US TERMINOLOGY	UK ABBREVIATIONS	UK TERMINOLOGY
blo	through back loops only	bl	through back loops only
ch	chain	ch	chain
dc	double crochet	tr	treble crochet
dc5tog	bobble stitch, double crochet 5 stitches together (or any number of stitches)	tr5tog	bobble stitch, treble crochet 5 stitches together (or any number of stitches)
dec	decrease	dec	decrease
flo	through front loops only	fl	through front loops only
hdc	half double crochet	htr	half treble crochet
inc	increase	inc	increase
rnd	round	rnd	round
sc	single crochet	dc	double crochet
sc3tog	single crochet 3 stitches together	dc3tog	double crochet 3 stitches together
sk st	skip stitch	-	miss
sl st	slip stitch	ss	slip stitch
sl st join	slip stitch join	ss join	slip stitch join
st	stitch	st	stitch

How to read a Woobles pattern

To read a crochet pattern, you need to decode the abbreviations and also understand what they mean when they're strung together. Every pattern designer writes patterns a little bit differently. Woobles patterns are written like this:

...

Do a stitch as many times as the # says. Each stitch should go into the next hole. If there's no number before the abbreviation, it means to do that stitch only once.

Example: 2 sc

Do a single crochet stitch in one hole. Then another single crochet stitch in the next.

TIP 2 sc is different from an increase stitch (inc). An increase stitch is two single crochet stitches in the same hole.

..., ...

Do each stitch separated by each comma in the next hole.

Example: sc, inc, hdc

Do a single crochet stitch in one hole. Then an increase stitch in the next hole. Then a half double crochet in the hole after that.

Example: 2 sc, inc

Do a single crochet stitch in one hole. Then another single crochet stitch in the next. Then an increase stitch in the hole after that.

[..., ...] x

Do the sequence in the brackets as many times as the # says.

Example: [2 sc, inc] x 6

Do the sequence in the brackets a total of 6 times. The sequence is: single crochet in the first hole, then single crochet in the next hole, then increase stitch in the next.

... in same st

Put all the stitches in the same hole

Example: 3 sc in same st

Put 3 single crochet stitches in the same hole.

(#)

At the end of each round, there's a number in parentheses. This is the total number of stitches–or horizontal Vs–you should have by the end of the round.

Example:

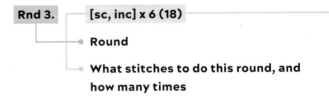

For round 3, repeat the sequence in the brackets 6 times. The sequence is: single crochet in the first hole, then increase stitch in the next. Because an increase stitch is actually two single crochet stitches in the same hole (see tutorial on page 30), it creates two horizontal V's and counts as two stitches. Therefore, the bracketed sequence represents 3 stitches repeated 6 times, for a total of 18 stitches in round 3.

TIP To catch any potential mistakes early on, get in the habit of counting how many horizontal Vs you have in a round at the end of each round. If it matches the number in the parentheses, you're good to go.

(color yarn)

If the pattern uses more than one color, the pattern will start with a color in parentheses. All stitches after this prompt should be crocheted in that color. When you come across the next color in parentheses, it means that all stitches after this prompt should be crocheted in that new color. But remember to introduce the new color in the last step of the previous stitch (see tutorial on page 50).

Example:

Rnd 1. (tan yarn) start 6 sc in magic loop (6)
Rnd 2. (switch to white yarn) 6 inc (12)

With tan yarn, make 6 single crochet stitches in a magic loop. With white yarn, make 6 increase stitches for round 2. Remember to introduce the white yarn in the last step of the last single crochet stitch in the magic loop.

Rnds #-#.

Crochet the same sequence of stitches for all of the rounds listed.

Example: Rnds 4–5. 8 sc (8)

For round 4, make 8 single crochet stitches. For round 5, make 8 single crochet stitches.

STITCHES

▶ Follow right- and left-handed video tutorials at **thewoobles.com/tutorials**

Before diving into the stitch tutorials, some things you should know:

- Always crochet with the yarn that's connected to the ball. This is called the "working yarn." The other end of the yarn is called a "tail."

- Always insert the hook under a stitch from the front to the back of the piece. It should look like you're pushing the hook away from you.

- You're done with a stitch when you only have one loop left on the hook.

- If you're right-handed, always crochet in the stitches to the left. If you're left-handed, always crochet in the stitches to the right.

- A "yarn over" is the basic technique used in every stitch. It goes like this:

  1. Put the hook in front of the working yarn, with the tip of the hook facing you.

  2. Bring the working yarn over the top of the hook so that the tip of the hook can grab onto it when moving on with the stitch.

  TIP Another way to think of this motion is to think of it as pushing the hook into the yarn.

TIP The direction you wrap the yarn around the hook matters. A "yarn over" is when you bring the yarn over the top of the hook. Don't confuse it with a "yarn under," which is when you bring the yarn under the bottom of the hook.

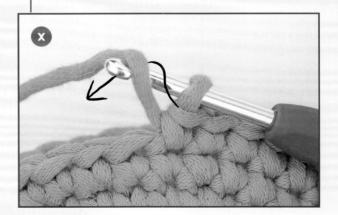

Slip stitch (sl st)

1. Insert the hook under the top loops of the next stitch.

2. Yarn over. Pull the yarn through the stitch and the loop on the hook to draw up a loop. There should be one loop left on the hook.

Single crochet (sc)

1. Insert the hook under the top loops of the next stitch.

2. Yarn over. Pull the yarn through the stitch to draw up a loop.

3. There should be two loops on the hook.

4. Yarn over. Pull the yarn through both loops on the hook. There should be one loop left on the hook.

Increase (inc)

An increase stitch is two single crochet stitches in the same hole.

1. Make the first sc by following steps 1-4 of the single crochet stitch (see tutorial on page 29).

2. Look for the hole that the first sc went into. It's the hole that the bottom of the vertical V you just made goes into.

3. Insert the hook into the hole.

4. Follow steps 2-4 of the single crochet stitch. The bottoms of the two vertical Vs you just made should trace back into the same hole.

TIP Having trouble figuring out what hole you just crocheted into? Take a look at the two loops of yarn that the yarn on your hook passes through. The loop that's closer to your yarn hand traces back into a hole. That's the hole you just crocheted into.

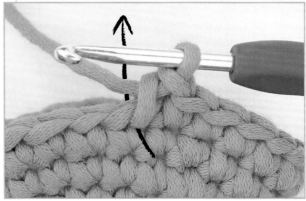

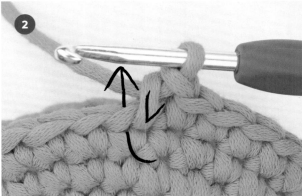

Decrease (dec)

There are two ways to crochet a decrease stitch. When working in the round, do the invisible decrease stitch for a smoother finish. When working on a piece where both the "right" and "wrong" sides of the piece will be visible, do the regular decrease stitch.

Invisible decrease stitch

1. Insert the hook under the front loop of the next stitch.

2. Insert the hook under front loop of the stitch after that.

3. Yarn over. Pull the yarn through both front loops to draw up a loop.

4. There should be two loops on the hook.

5. Yarn over. Pull the yarn through both loops on the hook. There should be one loop left on the hook.

> **TIP** It can be tricky to see where to put the hook after a dec. The telltale sign is the front loop. If you see that the front loop of a stitch has been pulled, that's part of the dec. The hook goes under the horizontal V next to that.

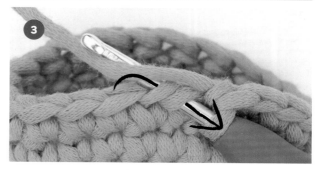

Regular decrease stitch

1. Insert the hook under the top loops of the next stitch.

2. Yarn over. Pull the yarn through the stitch to draw up a loop.

3. There should be two loops on the hook.

4. Insert the hook under the top loops of the next stitch.

5. Yarn over. Pull the yarn through the stitch to draw up a loop.

6. There should be three loops on the hook.

7. Yarn over. Pull the yarn through all three loops on the hook. There should be one loop left on the hook.

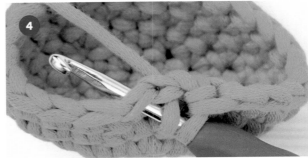

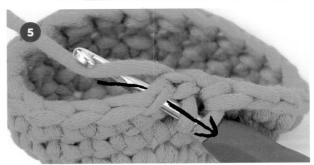

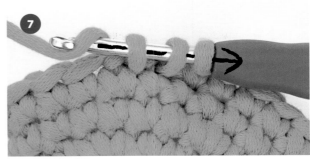

Chain (ch)

If a chain stitch is the first stitch in a pattern, that's your cue to make a "foundation chain." The only difference between a foundation chain and a regular chain stitch is that it starts with a slip knot (see tutorial on page 46).

To make a chain stitch, yarn over. Pull the yarn through the loop on hook. There should be one loop left on the hook.

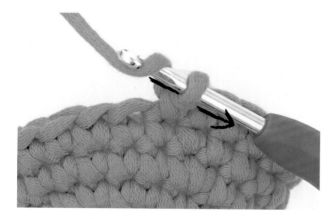

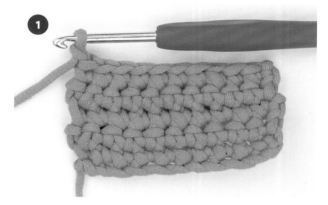

TIP Minimize the chance of twisting your chain by constantly moving your left hand to hold the chain as close as possible to the hook.

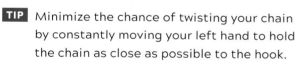

Chain 1 and turn (ch 1 and turn)

Because you always crochet in the same direction, you need to turn your work every time you finish a row so that there's something to crochet into again.

1. Make a chain stitch (see tutorial above).

2. Flip your piece like the page of a book, until your piece is on the other side of the loop on the hook.

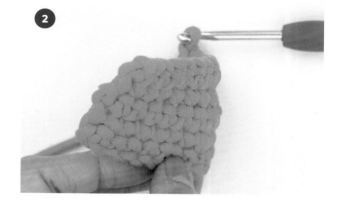

3. For the next stitch, put the hook under the top loops of the stitch two stitches away from the hook.

TIP The ch in the "ch 1 and turn" is just there to add height to the row. It doesn't count as a stitch, so it isn't added to the total number of stitches in the row.

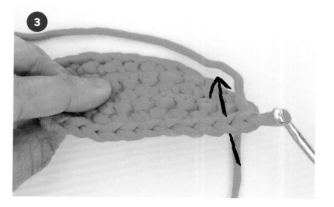

Half double crochet (hdc)

1. Yarn over.

2. Insert the hook under top loops of next stitch.

3. Yarn over. Pull the yarn through the stitch to draw up a loop.

4. There should be three loops on the hook.

5. Yarn over. Pull the yarn through all three loops on the hook. There should be one loop left on the hook.

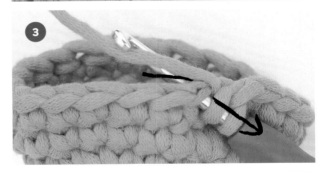

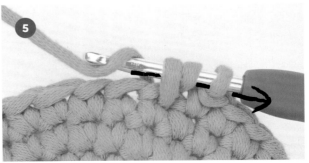

Double crochet (dc)

1. Yarn over.

2. Insert the hook under the top loops of the next stitch.

3. Yarn over. Pull the yarn through the stitch to draw up a loop.

4. There should be three loops on the hook.

5. Yarn over. Pull the yarn through only the first two loops on the hook.

6. There should be two loops left on the hook.

7. Yarn over. Pull the yarn through both loops on the hook. There should be one loop left on the hook.

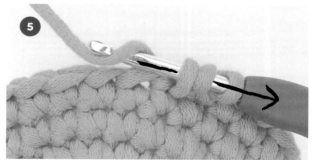

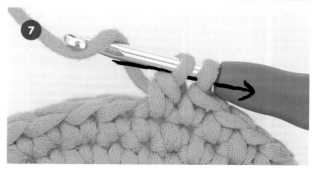

Bobble stitch or double crochet 5 stitches together (dc5tog)

1. Follow steps 1-6 of the double crochet stitch (see tutorial on page 35) so that there are two loops left on the hook. You've completed the first dc of five.

2. Yarn over.

3. Insert the hook in the same hole that the first dc went into.

TIP Can't find the hole? See increase tutorial on page 30 for a tip on how to find the hole.

4. Yarn over. Pull the yarn through the stitch to draw up a loop.

5. There should be four loops on the hook.

6. Yarn over. Pull the yarn through only the first two loops on the hook.

7. There should be three loops left on the hook.

8. Repeat steps 2-6 three more times, until you have six loops on the hook.

9. Yarn over. Pull the yarn through all six loops on the hook.

10. There should be one loop left on the hook. Make sure the final bump faces the outside of your work.

TIP If you need to double crochet together a different number of stitches, just change the number of times you repeat steps 2-7. You want to end with one more loop on the hook than the number of dc you're crocheting together. For example, to dc4tog, stop when you have five loops on the hook.

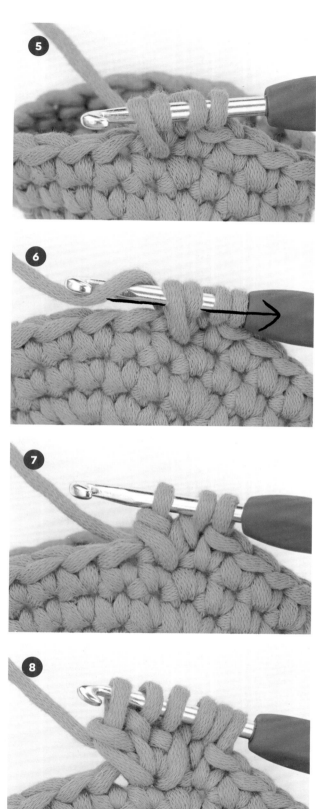

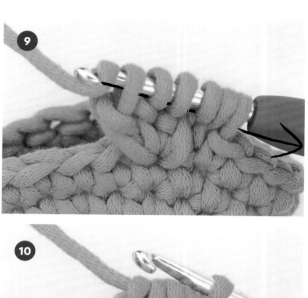

Single crochet 3 stitches together (sc3tog)

1. Insert the hook under the top loops of the next stitch.

2. Yarn over. Pull the yarn through the stitch to draw up a loop.

3. There should be two loops on the hook.

4. Repeat steps 1-2 two more times, until you have four loops on the hook.

5. Yarn over. Pull the yarn through all four loops on the hook. There should be one loop left on the hook.

TECHNIQUES

TIP Follow right- and left-handed video tutorials at **thewoobles.com/tutorials**

Undo stitches

1. Identify the stitch you want to keep.

2. With your right hand, hold onto the top loops of the stitch you want to keep.

3. With your left hand, slowly pull on the working yarn until the only loop left is the loop coming out of the stitch you want to keep.

4. Put the hook in this loop to continue crocheting.

TIP When you first feel a stitch coming undone, you'll probably be left with at least two loops. This means you haven't undone the whole stitch yet! Keep pulling until you only have one loop left. That loop should come out of the stitch you want to keep.

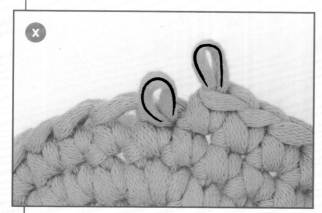

Magic loop

A magic loop, also called a magic ring or magic circle, is the preferred way to start crocheting in the round. It's considered magical because the result has no hole in the middle. It can be tricky to master so if you're having a lot of trouble with it, start a round piece with a chain instead (see tutorial on page 44).

1. Turn your left palm to face you. Hold the yarn tail in your right hand and place the yarn in front of your left palm.

2. Wrap the working yarn once around your pinky, so that the yarn tail ends up behind your hand.

3. Bring the yarn tail up the back of your hand until you can drape it over your pointer finger.

4. Loop it once around your pointer finger, so it crosses in front of your finger.

5. Hold onto the intersection with your left thumb and slide the loop off your finger using your right hand.

6. Insert the hook through the middle of the loop, from the front to the back.

7. Rotate the hook so the tip is facing away from you, and grab onto the working yarn.

8. Pull the working yarn back through the loop, while rotating the hook so that the tip faces you again, to draw up a loop. If you need more tension in the working yarn, move your middle finger away from you.

9. The hook should be in front of the working yarn.

10. Yarn over. Pull the yarn through the loop on the hook. There should be one loop left on the hook.

> **TIP** You just made a chain stitch in step 10. This does **not** count as a sc in the magic loop.

If you can let go of the magic loop and everything stays intact, you've done it correctly. Huzzah!

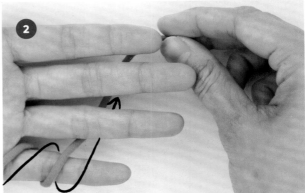

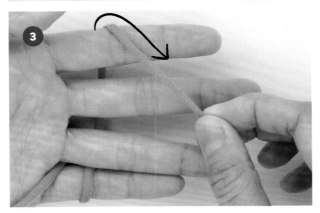

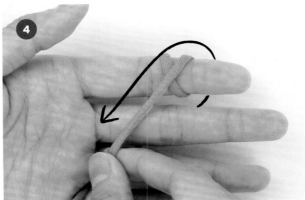

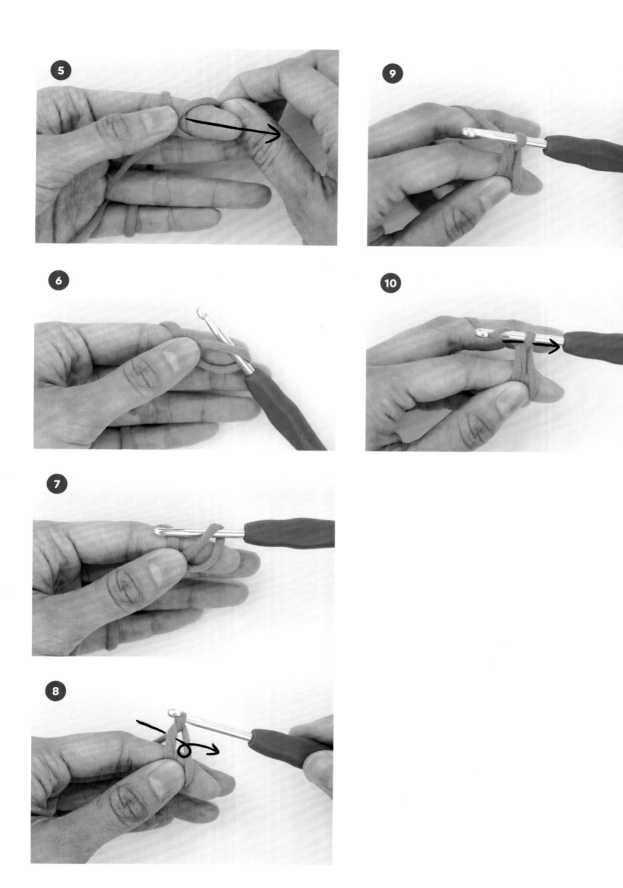

Single crochet in a magic loop

Now that you have a magic loop you can safely let go of, feel free to rearrange your grip to however you normally hold yarn.

1. With your left hand, hold onto both the left and right sides of the magic loop and the yarn tail. Keep the yarn tail on the left side of the magic loop.

2. Insert the hook through the middle of the loop, from the front to the back. The hook should look like it's under the left side of the loop and the yarn tail.

3. Yarn over. Pull the yarn back through the loop, under both the left side of the loop and the yarn tail, to draw up a loop.

4. There should be two loops on the hook.

5. Yarn over. Pull through both loops on the hook. There should be one loop left on the hook. This completes one sc.

TIP Make it easier to find the first stitch of the magic loop later, by putting a stitch marker under the top loops of this first stitch the moment you make it.

6. Repeat steps 2-5 until you have as many sc as the pattern calls for.

7. When you're done, put the hook down. With your right hand, hold onto the top loops of the stitches you just made. With your left hand, pull on the yarn tail until the magic loop disappears.

8. To start the next round, put the hook under the top loops of the stitch to the left.

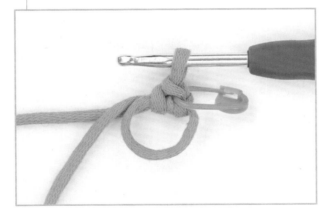

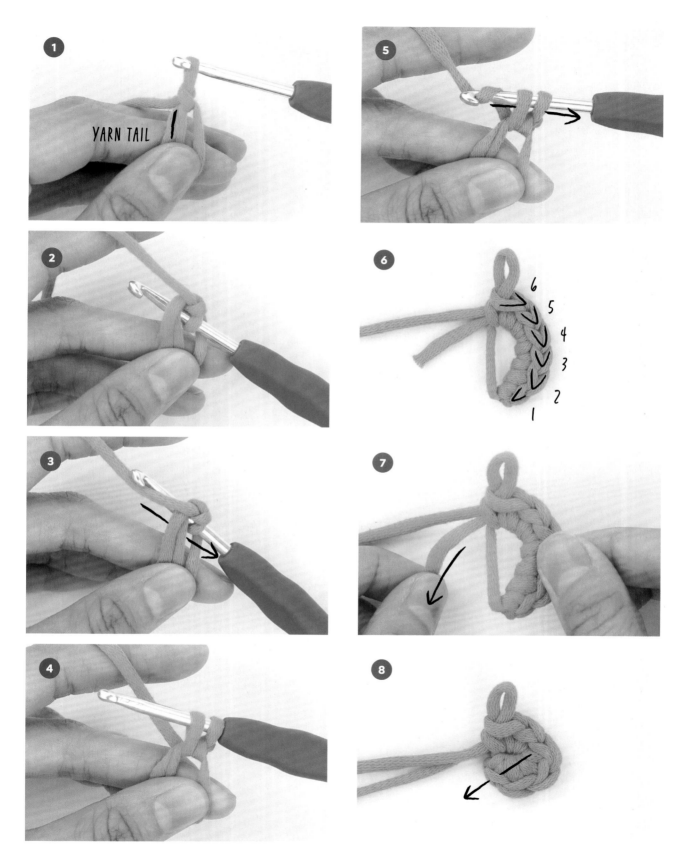

YARN TAIL

Start a round piece with a chain

Magic loop giving you trouble? Try this method instead.

1. Make a foundation chain with 4 ch in it (see tutorial on page 33). The tighter you can make these stitches, the smaller the hole in the middle of the final circle will be.

2. Bend the chain into a tiny U. Insert the hook under the front loop of the first ch, from the inside to the outside of the U.

3. Yarn over. Pull the yarn through both loops on the hook. There should be one loop left on the hook. This turns the tiny U into a tiny O.

4. Now you'll start crocheting as many sc as the pattern calls for into this tiny circle. Pull on both sides of the chain to find the hole in the middle of the circle you just made. Insert the hook through the middle hole, from the front to the back.

> **TIP** To help you see the center of the circle, as you add stitches to it, put a stitch marker in it.

5. Yarn over. Pull the yarn back through the middle hole to draw up a loop.

6. There should be two loops on the hook.

7. Yarn over. Pull the yarn through both loops on the hook. There should be one loop left on the hook. This completes one sc.

8. Repeat steps 4-7 until you have as many sc as the pattern calls for.

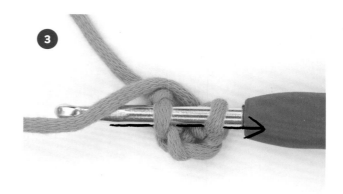

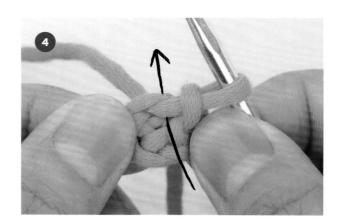

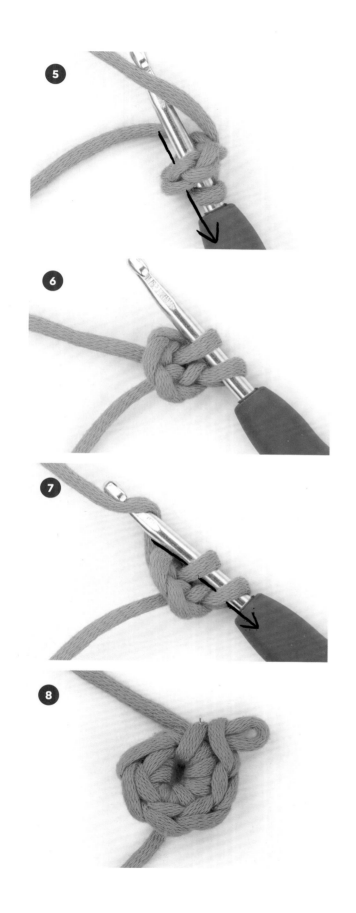

Slip knot

1. Lay the yarn out horizontally on a table, with the yarn tail on the right.

2. Cross the yarn tail over the working yarn.

3. Pick up the right side of the loop and flip it over the crossing point. The working yarn should be behind the middle of the loop.

4. Pick up the working yarn in the middle of the loop with your right hand.

5. Pull on the yarn tail with your left hand until a slip knot forms.

6. Put the loop on the hook, with the knot to the left of the hook. Pull on the working yarn to make the loop smaller.

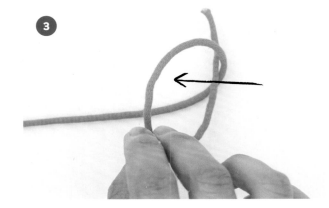

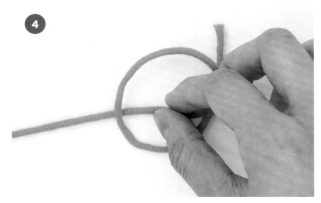

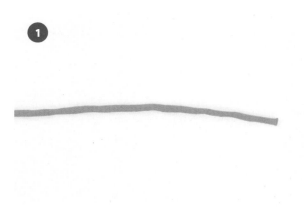

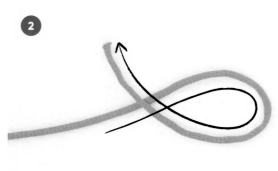

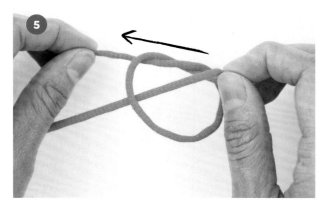

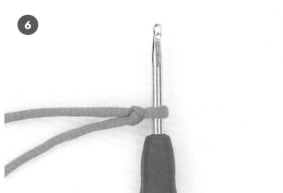

Crochet in rows

When crocheting in rows, there's a few things that patterns don't mention because they assume crocheters know what to do:

1. Start with a foundation chain (see tutorial on page 33).

2. To start the next row, skip the first ch from the hook. Insert the hook under the back loop of the second ch from the hook.

3. Crochet all stitches of this second row through the back loops of the foundation chain.

4. When you reach the end of the row, ch 1 and turn (see tutorial on page 33).

5. Remember that the first stitch of a new row gets crocheted into the second stitch from the hook. The hook should also go under both top loops of the previous row.

6. Repeat steps 4-5 until you finish the pattern.

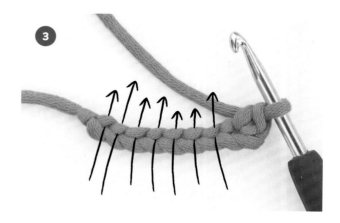

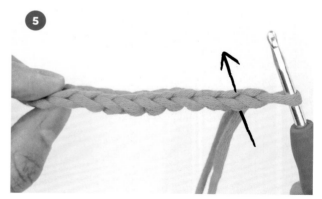

Start an oval

If a pattern tells you to rotate your foundation chain and crochet on the other side of the chain, that's code for: crochet an oval.

1. Crochet a foundation chain with as many ch as the pattern calls for.

2. Follow the pattern's instructions for the next row. Remember that the first sc goes under the back loop of the second ch from the hook, and that all stitches in a foundation chain go through the back loops only.

> **TIP** To help you stay oriented, put a stitch marker under the first sc.

3. At some point, the pattern will tell you to crochet a bunch of stitches in the last stitch of the foundation chain, and then rotate the piece so you can work on the other side of the foundation chain. Rotate the piece clockwise, until the other side of the foundation chain is facing up.

4. Crochet the rest of the round under the unworked front loops of the foundation chain.

5. This is what an oval that started with 4 ch looks like.

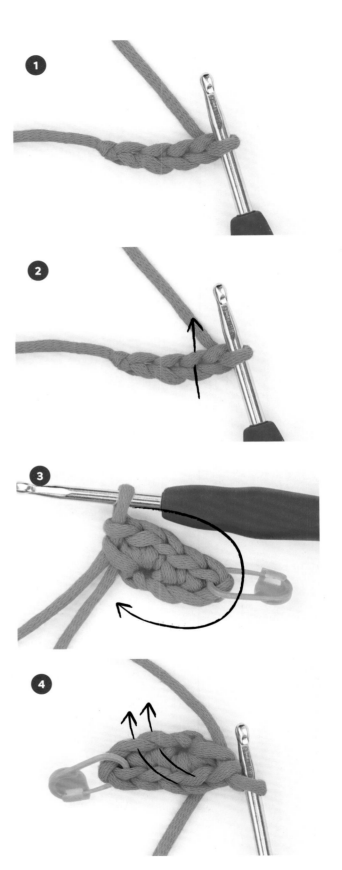

Change colors

1. For the stitch before the pattern says to switch colors, crochet it like normal until right before you get to the last yarn over. In this example, the stitch before the color change is a sc, so pause when you have two loops of color A on the hook.

2. Take color B and drape it on the hook. Leave at least a 6-inch yarn tail. The yarn tail should be on the side of the hook closer to you.

3. Pinch the yarn with your left hand to help give it enough tension so you can pull color B through the loops on the hook.

> **TIP** If this made the last loop of color A too big, pull on color A's working yarn.

4. There should be one loop of color B left on the hook.

5. Insert the hook under the top loops of the next stitch, plus color A's working yarn and Color B's tail.

6. Crochet the stitch written in the pattern like normal, using color B's working yarn. Every time you're supposed to yarn over and pull the yarn through a stitch to draw up a loop, remember to pull the working yarn under any unused yarn *and* through the stitch.

7. Every time you're supposed to yarn over and pull the yarn through loops on the hook, remember to do this above the unused yarn.

8. For at least the next 10 stitches, keep crocheting over color A's working yarn and color B's tail.

9. If you're going to use color A in the same or next round, keep crocheting over it. If not, cut it as close to the piece as possible.

10. To switch back to color A, crochet the stitch before the pattern says to switch colors, and pause before you do the last yarn over.

11. Yarn over with color A. Pull color A through the loops on the hook so you're left with one loop of color B.

12. Continue following the pattern, this time crocheting with color A and crocheting over color B.

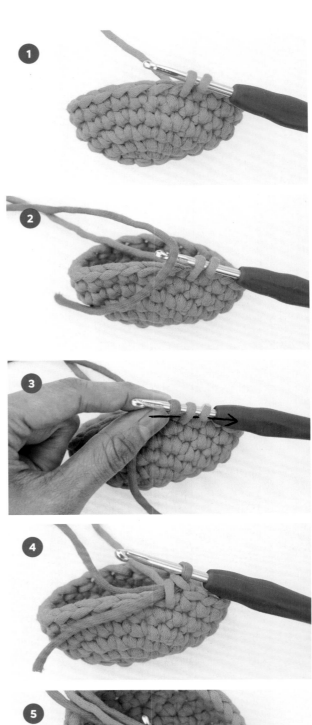

EVERYTHING YOU NEED TO KNOW

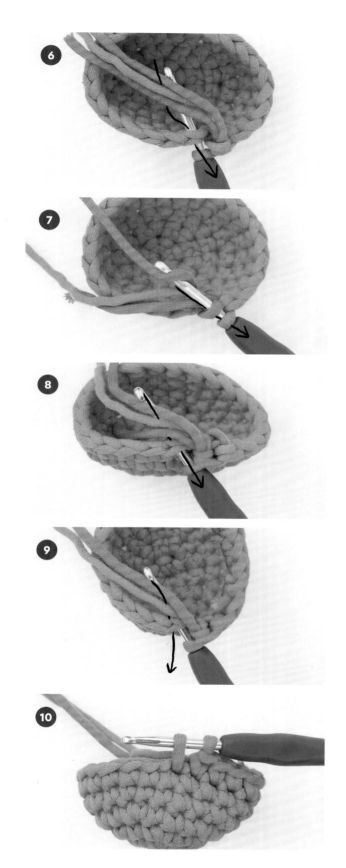

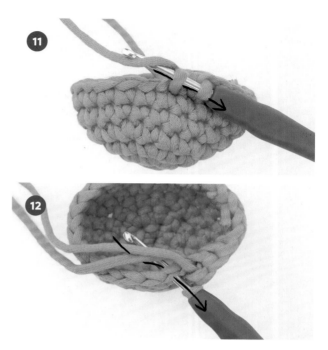

TIP To minimize the chance of the unused color peeking out, hold the unused color's working yarn on the inside of the piece.

Add another yarn ball

If you've used up all your yarn, add a new ball of yarn to keep on crocheting. This is called "joining" yarn. Follow steps 1-9 of changing colors (see tutorial on page 50), but instead of introducing a new color, introduce a new yarn ball.

Add safety eyes

Safety eyes are ironically not safe for small children or pets. You can always embroider eyes instead (see tutorial on page 56).

1. Safety eyes come with an eye and a backing.

2. Make sure the "right side" of the piece is facing you (see tutorial on page 22). Insert the eye between two stitches.

3. On the inside of the piece, put the backing on the stem, flat side facing the yarn.

4. Push down on both sides of the backing to snap it into place. Push it far enough that it's secure, but not so far that it distorts the piece.

5. Repeat steps 2-4 for the other eye. Count how many stitches away the second eye should be by counting the number of gaps that represent the space between stitches.

TIP Before putting the backings on, put both safety eyes where the pattern instructs. Then adjust their placement if you think it could look better.

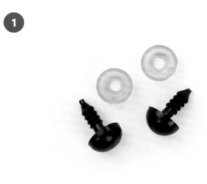

Stuff amigurumi

How you stuff an amigurumi greatly affects its final shape: lumpy or smooth, saggy or plump. If you don't add enough, your amigurumi might sink in here or there. But if you add too much, you'll be able to see the stuffing from the outside. Here's what the same pattern looks like when stuffed too little, just right, and too much, from left to right.

It takes some time to learn how much stuffing is the right amount. Keep checking how it looks as you slowly add more stuffing in layers:

1. Pull apart a thin layer of stuffing. Shape it so that it's about the same diameter as the bottom of the piece.

2. Tuck this layer of stuffing into the piece. Push down on all angles, even on the edges, to make it as flat as possible.

3. Repeat steps 1-2 until you've filled the whole piece, adjusting the diameter of the stuffing layer to match what you're currently filling.

TOO LITTLE   JUST RIGHT   TOO MUCH

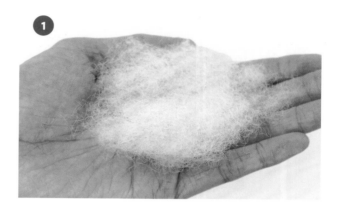

Close a ball

1. Finish the last stitch and cut the yarn so that the yarn tail is at least 6 inches long.

2. Pull the remaining loop until there's no loop left.

3. Thread a needle with the yarn tail. If you have a gap in the middle of the ball, insert the needle through the front loops of each stitch from the bottom up. Pull tight each time you bring the needle through a loop.

4. Hide the yarn tail in the piece (see tutorial on page 55) by putting the needle through the middle of the circle you just closed and out some other point on the piece.

Hide yarn tails

When you're done with a 3D piece, make sure the yarn won't unravel by hiding the yarn tails:

1. Thread a needle with the yarn tail of the last stitch. Insert the needle into the hole that the yarn tail came out of.

2. Pull it out on the other side of the piece. Tug as hard as you need to, to hide the yarn inside the piece.

3. Cut the yarn tail as close to the piece as possible. Then massage the piece until the yarn tail disappears inside the piece.

Embroider eyes

Finish the piece that'll be embroidered onto.

1. Thread a needle with an arm's length of black yarn. Insert the needle somewhere on the right side of the amigurumi, and out where you want the bottom of the right eye to be. Leave a 6-inch yarn tail.

2. Insert the needle one round up and pull it out the same bottom point of the right eye.

TIP Be careful not to pull the yarn too tight, otherwise the stuffing might be visible above and below the eye.

3. Repeat step 2 until the eye is as big as you want, probably at least four times. To make the other eye, insert the needle into the top of the current eye, and pull it out where you want the bottom of the second eye to be.

4. Repeat step 2 until the eye is as big as you want. To finish, insert the needle into the top of the current eye and pull it out from the same hole it originally went in, so that both yarn tails are coming out of the same hole.

5. Tie a knot with both yarn tails, as close to the surface of the piece as possible. Hide the yarn tails in the piece (see tutorial on page 55).

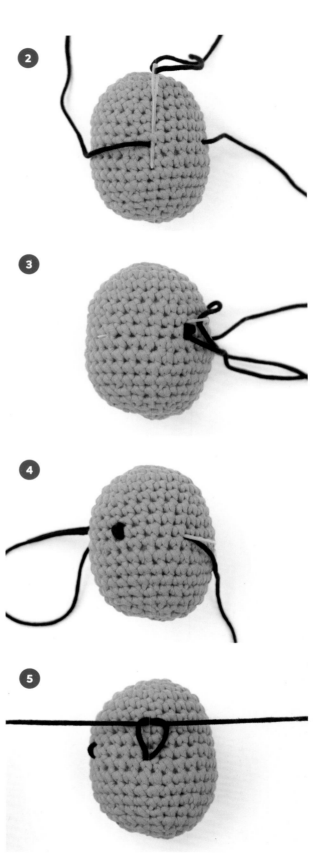

Embroider blush

Finish the piece that'll be embroidered onto.

1. Thread a needle with an arm's length of pink yarn. Insert the needle somewhere on the right side of the amigurumi, and out under the left side of the right eye. Leave a 6-inch yarn tail.

2. Insert the needle one stitch to the right, and out under the left side of the left eye.

> **TIP** Be careful not pull the yarn too tight, otherwise the stuffing might be visible around the blush.

3. Insert the needle one stitch to the right and pull it out the same hole where it originally went in, so that both yarn tails are coming out of the same hole.

4. Tie a knot with both yarn tails, as close to the surface of the piece as possible. Hide the yarn tails in the piece (see tutorial on page 55).

Embroider a curve

Finish the piece that'll be embroidered onto.

1. Thread a needle with an arm's length of black yarn. Insert the needle somewhere on the right side of the amigurumi, and out where you want the right end of the curve to be. Leave a 6-inch yarn tail.

2. Insert the needle where you want the left side of the curve to be, and out where you want the bottom of the curve to be.

3. Pull the yarn just tight enough so that the curve looks like how you want it.

4. Make sure the needle and yarn came out below the curve. Then bring the needle up and over the curve, and insert the needle in the same hole it just came out of. Pull tight to secure the curve.

5. Pull the needle out of the same hole in the piece it originally went into, so that both yarn tails are coming out of the same hole.

6. Tie a knot with both yarn tails, as close to the surface of the piece as possible. Hide the yarn tails in the piece (see tutorial on page 55).

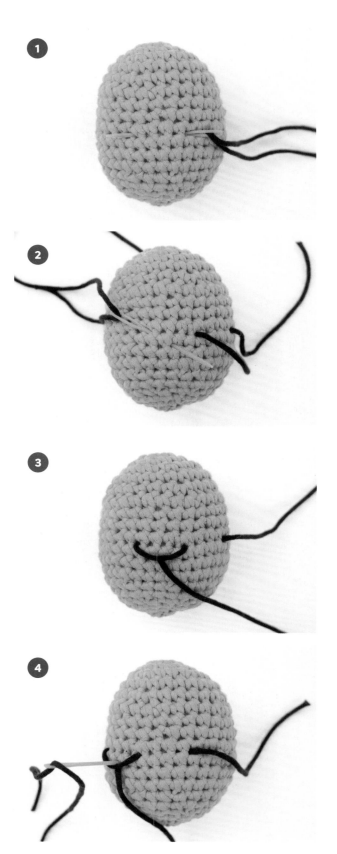

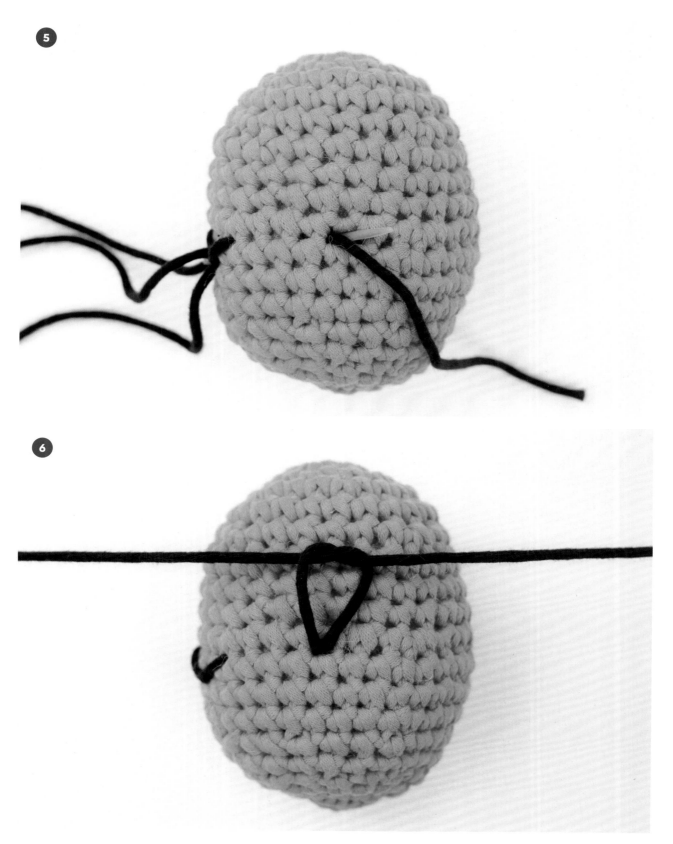

Embroider a nose and mouth

Finish the piece that'll be embroidered onto.

1. Thread a needle with an arm's length of black yarn. Insert the needle somewhere on the right side of the amigurumi, and out where you want the left side of the nose to be. Leave a 6-inch yarn tail.

2. Insert the needle where you want the right side of the nose to be, and out below the nose, centered between the left and right sides of the nose.

3. Insert the needle between the left and right points of the nose. Pull it out on the left side of the nose.

4. Insert the needle in the right side of the nose, and out the left side of the nose.

5. Repeat step 4 until the nose is as big as you want, probably at least 4 times.

6. Insert the needle in the right side of the nose and pull it out the same hole in the piece it originally went into, so that both yarn tails are coming out of the same hole.

7. Tie a knot with both yarn tails, as close to the surface of the piece as possible. Hide the yarn tails in the piece (see tutorial on page 55).

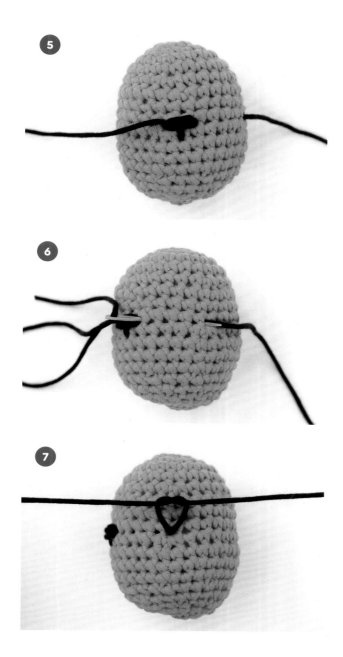

Invisible fasten off

For pieces that'll be sewed onto another, or for a piece where the edge will be seen, you can use a technique called the "invisible fasten off." This technique makes the edge look smooth.

1. Finish the last stitch and cut the yarn so that the yarn tail is at least 6 inches longer than the circumference of the rim of the piece.

2. Pull the hook away from the piece until there's no loop left on the hook. Thread a needle with the yarn tail.

3. Skip the next stitch. Insert the needle under the top loops of the stitch after that, from the outside to the inside of the piece.

4. Before pulling it tight, insert the needle under the back loop of the stitch the yarn tail came out from.

5. Pull the yarn tail tight enough so that the loop you've just created is the same size as the other stitches along the rim.

Sew something flat onto another piece

1. Invisible fasten off the flat piece (Piece A) (see tutorial on page 62). Hold Piece A on top of the other piece (Piece B), with the "right side" visible (see tutorial on page 22).

2. Thread a needle with Piece A's yarn tail from the invisible fasten off. Insert the needle into Piece B right under the point where the yarn tail came out from. Pull it out of Piece B one stitch over, following the edge of the Piece A. Pull the yarn tight after every step.

> **TIP** Use pins to hold Piece A in place as you sew it on.

3. Insert the needle under the top loops of Piece A from the bottom up, directly above where it came out of Piece B.

4. Insert the needle under the top loops of the next stitch of Piece A from the top down.

5. Insert the needle into Piece B, directly below where it came out of Piece A. Pull it out of Piece B one stitch over, following the edge of Piece A.

6. Repeat steps 3-5 until all of Piece A is sewn onto Piece B. To finish, hide the yarn tail in the piece (see tutorial on page 55).

Sew amigurumi parts together

1. Invisible fasten off the piece being sewn on (Piece A).

2. Hold Piece A on top of the other piece (Piece B), with the "right side" visible (see tutorial on page 22). Thread a needle with Piece A's yarn tail from the invisible fasten off. Insert the needle into Piece B right under the point where the yarn tail came out from. Pull it out of Piece B one stitch over, following the edge of the Piece A. Pull the yarn tight after every step.

> **TIP** Use pins to hold Piece A in place as you sew it on.

3. Insert the needle under the top loops of Piece A from the bottom up, directly above where it came out of Piece B.

4. Bring the needle over the top loops of the same stitch on Piece A and insert it into the same hole it just came out of.

5. Pull it out of Piece B one stitch over, following the edge of Piece A.

6. Repeat steps 3-5 until all of Piece A is sewn onto Piece B. To finish, hide the yarn tail in the piece (see tutorial on page 55).

Fasten off

When you've finished the last stitch, patterns will often tell you to "fasten off leaving a long tail." A long yarn tail is usually at least 6 inches long, or if you're sewing the piece onto something else, at least the length of the current piece's edge. Fastening off keeps the piece together.

1. Finish the last stitch, then yarn over. Pull the yarn through the loop on the hook. There should be one loop left on the hook.

2. Cut the yarn at least 6 inches away from the intersection point.

3. Keep pulling the yarn all the way through the loop until you have a knot. If you're done crocheting a flat piece, weave in the yarn tails (see tutorial on page 67).

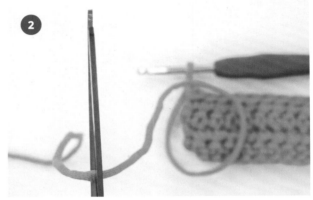

Weave in ends

When you're done crocheting a flat piece and fastening off, make sure your yarn doesn't unravel by weaving in both yarn tails.

1. With the wrong side of the piece facing you, thread a needle with the yarn tail. Insert it through a few stitches of the last row and pull the yarn through.

2. Skip the last vertical piece of yarn the needle just went under and insert the needle through the same stitches in the opposite direction.

3. Cut the yarn tail as close as possible to the piece and massage the piece until the yarn tail disappears.

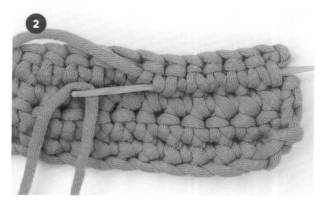

Whip stitch

Even though it's called a stitch, a "whip stitch" is a sewing technique that uses a needle. It's used to sew two edges with the same number of stitches together. For this technique, always pull the needle through stitches in the same direction.

1. Thread a needle with the yarn tail. Line up the two edges that'll be sewn together. Insert the needle under the top loops of the other piece's edge, starting from the same end as the yarn tail. Remember to pull tight after every whip stitch.

2. Insert the needle under the top loops of the next pair of stitches on opposite pieces. Remember to insert the needle in the same direction as the previous step. Pull yarn through.

3. Repeat step 2 until you've whip stitched together all the top loops. Weave in the yarn tail on the "wrong side" of the piece (see tutorial on page 22).

Slip stitch join (sl st join)

1. Make a slip knot and put it on the hook (see tutorial on page 46). Insert the hook under the top loops of the stitch where you'll be making the sl st join.

2. Yarn over. Pull the yarn through the stitch and the loop on the hook to draw up a loop. There should be one loop left on the hook.

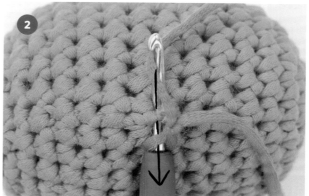

ENGAGEMENT

FINAL SIZE

Height: 4 in / 10.2 cm
Width: 3 in / 7.6 cm

YARN

The Woobles Easy Peasy Yarn
or any medium-weight #4 yarn
Yellow: What's Up Buttercup,
80 yds / 73 m
Brown: A Whole Latte Love,
2 yds / 2 m
Green: Leaf It to Us, 2 yd / 2 m
Pink: Eat, Pink & Be Merry,
2 yd / 2 m

CROCHET HOOK

US G-6 / 4mm

OTHER MATERIALS

- Two pairs of 10mm black safety eyes
- Stuffing
- Stitch marker
- Tapestry needle

VIDEOS

▶ thewoobles.com/celebrate

PYRUS AND LI THE PEARS

The Perfect Pear

Pre-pear yourself for the cutest little fruits you ever did see—which happen to make an ideal gift for that pear-y special couple. Whether they just got engaged, recently tied the knot, or made it to a milestone anniversary, they're sure to find these sweet little pears a-peel-ing. In fact, we think they're pretty much pear-fect!

BODY

With yellow yarn (make two).

TIP Keep track of where you are by placing a stitch marker in the first stitch of the current round. See tutorial on page 24.

Rnd 1.	start 6 sc in magic loop (6)
Rnd 2.	6 inc (12)
Rnd 3.	[sc, inc] x 6 (18)
Rnd 4.	[inc, 2 sc] x 6 (24)
Rnds 5-6.	24 sc (24)
Rnd 7.	[4 sc, dec] x 4 (20)
Rnd 8.	20 sc (20)
Rnd 9.	[inc, sc] x 10 (30)
Rnd 10.	30 sc (30)
Rnd 11.	[14 sc, inc] x 2 (32)
Rnds 12-13.	32 sc (32)
Rnd 14.	[2 sc, dec] x 8 (24)
Rnd 15.	24 sc (24)
Rnd 16.	[dec, sc] x 8 (16)
Rnd 17.	16 sc (16)

Attach the eyes between rounds 8 and 9, with a 4-stitch space between them. If this amigurumi is for a baby or pet, embroider the eyes instead (see tutorial on page 56). Stuff the piece.

Rnd 18.	8 dec (8)

Fasten off leaving a long tail. Thread a needle with the tail. Use it to pull the yarn tail through the front loops of each stitch. Pull tight to close the remaining gap.

STEM

With brown yarn (make two, one on each pear).

Row 1.   ch 5 (5)

TIP When crocheting a new row, remember to skip the first stitch from the hook. And for the first row after a chain, remember to crochet under the back loops only. See tutorial on page 47.

Row 2.   4 sl st (4)

Fasten off leaving a long tail (at least three times the height of the pear). Use this tail to embroider an "X" at the bottom of the pear and secure the stem to the pear:

Step 1.
To begin the embroidery, thread a needle with the tail. Insert the needle down through the middle of the pear, from the top to the bottom. Pull the needle out a little off-center from the middle of the bottom, leaving a 6-inch yarn tail.

Step 2.
Embroider one side of an "X" at the bottom of the pear. Insert the needle a little down and to the right, and out about one stitch left.

Step 3.
Embroider the other side of the "X." Insert the needle up and to the right, to make the upper right point of the "X." Pull the needle out the middle of the top of the pear.

Step 4.
Secure the bottom of the stem to the pear by inserting the needle through the bottom of the stem and then back down into the middle of the pear. Pull until it feels secure; then hide both yarn tails.

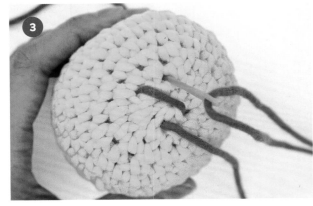

LEAF

With green yarn (make two, one on each pear).

Row 1. ch 5 (5)

Row 2. sl st, hdc, dc, sl st (4)

Fasten off leaving a long tail. Thread a needle with the tail. Use it to sew on the leaf where the stem meets the pear. For one pear, sew the leaf to the right side. For the other, sew the leaf to the left side.

BLUSH

With pink yarn (make one on each pear).

Thread a needle with an arm's length of yarn. Use it to embroider blush under each eye, between rounds 9 and 10.

TIP See tutorial for embroidering blush on page 57.

FINAL SIZE

Height: 1 in / 3.8 cm

Width: 5 in / 12.7 cm

YARN

The Woobles Easy Peasy Yarn

or any medium-weight #4 yarn

Green: Leaf It to Us, 50 yds / 46 m

Black: The Coal Shebang, 1 yd / 1 m

White: Snow Place Like Home,
1 yd / 1 m

Pink: Eat, Pink & Be Merry,
1 yd / 1 m

CROCHET HOOK

US G-6 / 4mm

OTHER MATERIALS

- Two pairs of 8mm black
  safety eyes
- Stuffing
- Stitch marker
- Tapestry needle

VIDEOS

 thewoobles.com/celebrate

SUGAR AND SNOW THE TWO PEAS IN A POD

For the Hap-pea Couple

Peanut butter and jelly. Tacos and Tuesdays. There are some pairings that were just meant to be. And this pod is a match made in heaven to celebrate married people, about-to-be-married people, partnered people, crocheting people, hope-to-be crocheting people, hungry people, crafty people, or people who just appreciate awesome stuff.

PEA

With green yarn (make two).

> **TIP** Keep track of where you are by placing a stitch marker in the first stitch of the current round. See tutorial on page 24.

Rnd 1.	start 6 sc in magic loop (6)
Rnd 2.	6 inc (12)
Rnd 3.	[sc, inc] x 6 (18)
Rnds 4-6.	18 sc (18)
Rnd 7.	[sc, dec] x 6 (12)

Attach the eyes between rounds 4 and 5, with a 4-stitch space between them. If this amigurumi is for a baby or pet, embroider the eyes instead (see tutorial on page 56). Stuff the piece.

Rnd 8.	6 dec (6)

Fasten off leaving a long tail. Thread a needle with the tail. Use it to pull the yarn tail through the front loops of each stitch. Pull tight to close the remaining gap.

BLUSH

With pink yarn (make one on each pea).

Thread a needle with an arm's length of yarn. Use it to embroider blush under each eye, between rounds 5 and 6.

 TIP See tutorial for embroidering blush on page 57.

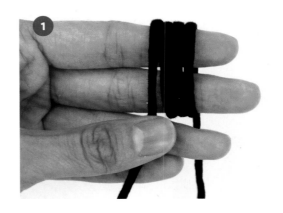

BOW

With white and black yarn (make one in each color, one color for one pea).

▶ Video tutorial at **thewoobles.com/celebrate**

Wrap the yarn into a bow before sewing it onto the pea:

Step 1.
With your left palm facing you, place the yarn tail in front of your palm. Wrap the yarn three times around your second and third fingers.

Step 2.
Hold the middle tightly and use your right hand to slide the loops off of your fingers. There should be three loops on each side.

Step 3.
Take the longer yarn tail and wrap it around the middle of the loops at least three times.

Step 4.
Tie a knot with both yarn tails.

Step 5.
Sew a bow onto each pea: thread a needle with one of the longer yarn tails. Insert the needle through the pea where you want the top middle of the bow to be and pull it out one stitch below. For a bowtie, sew the bow onto the bottom of the pea, centered between the eyes. For a bow headpiece, sew the bow on at a 45-degree angle above one of the eyes.

Step 6.
Bring the needle over the middle of the bow and pull it in and out of the same spots until it feels secure. Then hide both yarn tails.

PEA POD

With green yarn.

Row 1.   ch 25 (25)

TIP When crocheting a new row, remember to skip the first stitch from the hook. And for the first row after a chain, remember to crochet under the back loops only. See tutorial on page 47.

Rows 2–15. 24 sc, ch 1 and turn (24)

Fasten off and weave in the tail.

Sew the ends of the piece together to create the pea pod shape:

▶ Video tutorial at **thewoobles.com/celebrate**

Step 1.
Lay the piece out so that the longer sides are on top and bottom.

Step 2.
Create a triangle on the right end of the pea pod by bringing the bottom right corner to meet the middle of the top edge.

Step 3.
Fold the upper left corner of the triangle to meet the upper right corner of the triangle. In the process, the bottom of the piece will begin to fold upward.

Step 4.
Bring the bottom edge to the top edge.

Step 5.
Thread a needle with a forearm's length of green yarn. Use it to sew the pea pod end together. Pull the needle through all four layers, as close as possible to the intersection point of all four layers. Leave a 6-inch tail.

Step 6.
Insert the needle one stitch behind and back through all four layers. Pull tight.

Step 7.
Keep pulling the needle in and out of all four layers through the same points until the pea pod end feels secure. Then, bring both yarn tails to the inside of the pod and weave them in on the inside of the pea pod.

Step 8.
Repeat steps 2-7 to sew together the other end of the pea pod.

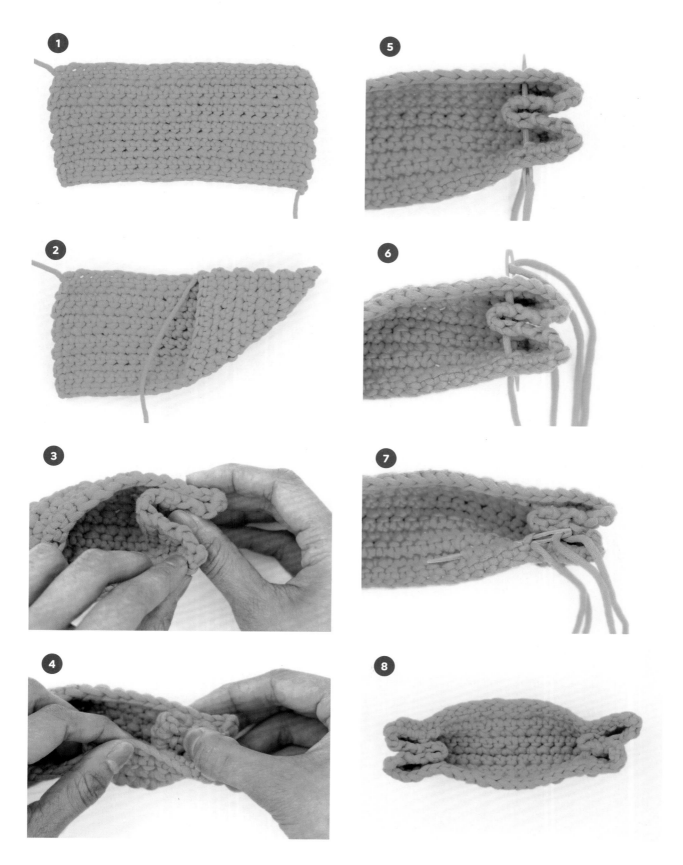

FINAL SIZE

Height: 4 in / 10.2 cm
Width: 4 in / 10.2 cm

YARN

The Woobles Easy Peasy Yarn
or any medium-weight #4 yarn
Color A: Green, Leaf It to Us *OR*
Orange, Orange You Glad,
40 yds / 36 m
Color B: Orange, Orange You
Glad *OR* Pink, Eat, Pink & Be
Merry, 20 yds / 55 m
Yellow: What's Up Buttercup,
2 yds / 2 m

CROCHET HOOK

US G-6 / 4mm

OTHER MATERIALS

 Two pairs of 10mm black
safety eyes
 Stuffing
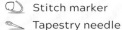 Stitch marker
 Tapestry needle

VIDEOS

thewoobles.com/celebrate

DAI AND SUKI THE LOVEBIRDS
For the Egg-cellent Duo

When it comes to celebrating the perfect couple, you don't want to wing it. But don't worry—these little lovebirds will take your gift-giving to the nest level. They adore whispering tweet nothings in each other's ears, and those feather-ific hearts make them irresistible. So let's raise a glass to the fowl-bulous couple!

HEAD AND BODY

With color A and color B yarn (make one in each color combination).

> **TIP** Keep track of where you are by placing a stitch marker in the first stitch of the current round. See page 24 for a tutorial.

Rnd 1.	(color A) start 6 sc in magic loop (6)
Rnd 2.	6 inc (12)
Rnd 3.	[sc, inc] x 6 (18)
Rnd 4.	[inc, 2 sc] x 6 (24)
Rnd 5.	24 sc (24)
Rnd 6.	[5 sc, inc] x 4 (28)
Rnds 7-9.	28 sc (28)
Rnd 10.	[6 sc, inc] x 4 (32)

> **TIP** You're changing colors in the next round. Remember to switch colors in the last step of the stitch before the color change. See tutorial on page 50.

Rnd 11. 13 sc, (switch to color B) 2 sc, (switch to color A) 2 sc, (switch to color B) 2 sc, (switch to color A) 13 sc (32)

> **TIP** To better hide the unused color, hide the unused color behind the color you're crocheting with.

Rnd 12. 12 sc, (switch to color B) 9 sc, (switch to color A) 11 sc (32)

Rnd 13. 13 sc, (switch to color B) 8 sc, (switch to color A) 11 sc (32)

Rnd 14. [2 sc, dec] x 3, 2 sc, (switch to color B) dec, 2 sc, dec, (switch to color A) [2 sc, dec] x 3 (24)

Rnd 15. 13 sc, (switch to color B) sc, (switch to color A) 10 sc (24)

Cut color B as close to the piece as possible. Attach the eyes between rounds 9 and 10, with a 6-stitch space between them. If this amigurumi is for a baby or pet, embroider the eyes instead (see tutorial on page 56). Stuff the piece, shaping it like an egg.

Rnd 16.   [sc, dec] x 8 (16)
Rnd 17.   16 sc (16)
Rnd 18.   8 dec (8)

Fasten off leaving a long tail. Thread a needle with the tail. Use it to pull the yarn tail through the front loops of each stitch. Pull tight to close the remaining gap.

WINGS

With color A yarn (make four total, two in each color for each lovebird).

Rnd 1.   start 4 sc in magic loop (4)
Rnd 2.   4 inc (8)
Rnd 3.   8 sc, ch 1 (8)

Single crochet the two sides of the open edge of each wing together:

Step 1.
Flatten the wing and insert the hook under the first two stiches across from each other. Sc.

Step 2.
Continue to sc together the next three pairs of stitches. Fasten off leaving a long tail.

Thread a needle with the tail. Use it to sew a wing on either side of each lovebird, three stitches back from the eyes and between rounds 11 and 12.

TAIL

With color A yarn (make one in each color, for each lovebird).

Rnd 1.   start 4 sc in magic loop (4)
Rnd 2.   4 sc (4)
Rnd 3.   4 inc (8)

Invisible fasten off leaving a long yarn tail. Thread a needle with the yarn tail. Use it to sew the love-bird's tail piece to the lower backside of the body, at round 14.

BEAK

With yellow yarn (make one on each lovebird).

Thread a needle with an arm's length of yarn. Embroider a beak between the eyes, spanning round 10.

> **TIP**   Use the same technique for the beak that you use to embroider eyes (see tutorial on page 56).

FINAL SIZE
Height: 4 in / 10.2 cm
Width: 4 in / 10.2 cm

YARN

The Woobles Easy Peasy Yarn
or any medium-weight #4 yarn
Brown: A Whole Latte Love,
80 yds / 73 m
Black: The Coal Shebang,
40 yds / 36 m
Tan: This Sand is Your Sand,
12 yds / 11 m
Green: Leaf It to Us, 6 yds / 6 m
Pink: Eat, Pink & Be Merry,
6 yds / 6 m
White: Snow Place Like Home,
6 yds / 6 m

CROCHET HOOK

US G-6 / 4mm

OTHER MATERIALS

 Two pairs of 10mm black
safety eyes
 Stuffing
 Stitch marker
 Tapestry needle

VIDEOS

▶ thewoobles.com/celebrate

SKIPPER AND BOOM THE OTTERS
Celebrate Your Otter Half

This is probably the cutest way ever to honor your significant otter. First of all, otters hold hands while they sleep. (Cue *aaaaw*). Second, that top hat and flower crown? Otter-ly amazing. And finally, you otter know that these work equally well for engagements, weddings, anniversaries, or just because. Huzzah!

HEAD AND BODY

With brown yarn (make two).

> **TIP** Keep track of where you are by placing a stitch marker in the first stitch of the current round. See tutorial on page 24.

Rnd 1.	start 6 sc in magic loop (6)
Rnd 2.	6 inc (12)
Rnd 3.	[sc, inc] x 6 (18)
Rnd 4.	[inc, 2 sc] x 6 (24)
Rnd 5.	24 sc (24)
Rnd 6.	[5 sc, inc] x 4 (28)
Rnds 7-9.	28 sc (28)
Rnd 10.	[6 sc, inc] x 4 (32)
Rnds 11-13.	32 sc (32)
Rnd 14.	[2 sc, dec] x 8 (24)
Rnd 15.	24 sc (24)
Rnd 16.	[sc, dec] x 8 (16)
Rnd 17.	16 sc (16)

> **TIP** Attach the eyes between rounds 7 and 8, with a 6-stitch space between them. If this amigurumi is for a baby or pet, embroider the eyes instead (see tutorial on page 56). Stuff the piece, shaping it like an egg.

Rnd 18.	8 dec (8)

Fasten off leaving a long tail. Thread the needle with the tail. Use it to pull the yarn tail through the front loops of each stitch. Pull tight to close the remaining gap.

EARS

With brown yarn (make four, two for each otter).

Rnd 1.   start 4 sc in magic loop (4)
Rnd 2.   4 inc (8)

Invisible fasten off leaving a long tail. Thread a needle with the tail. Use it to sew two ears onto the sides of each otter head, spanning rounds 4 to 6.

TAIL

With brown yarn (make two).

Rnd 1.   start 4 sc in magic loop (4)
Rnd 2.   [sc, inc] x 2 (6)
Rnds 3–6. 6 sc (6)
Rnd 7.   [inc, 2 sc] x 2 (8)

Invisible fasten off leaving a long yarn tail. Thread a needle with the yarn tail. Use it to sew the otter's tail piece to the middle backside of each otter, at round 15.

SNOUT

With tan yarn (make four pieces, two for each snout).

Rnd 1.   start 6 sc in magic loop (6)

Invisible fasten off leaving a long tail. Thread a needle with the tail. Use it to sew two of the snout circles between the eyes of each otter, spanning rounds 8 to 9.

NOSE

With black yarn (make one on each otter).

Fill in the top space between the two circles of the snout with an embroidered upside-down triangle:

Step 1.
To start the embroidery, thread a needle with an arm's length of yarn. Insert the needle on the right side of the body, and out the top of the left snout circle. Leave a 6-inch tail.

Step 2.
Insert the needle where the two circles meet. Pull it out the top of the right snout circle.

Step 3.
Insert the needle where the two circles meet. Pull it out the top left point of the nose.

Step 4.
Insert the needle into the top right point of the nose. Pull it out slightly to the right of the top left point of the nose.

Step 5.
Fill in the nose by inserting the needle in the bottom point of the nose and pulling it out slightly to the right of the last point on the top edge of the nose.

Step 6.
Once the nose is completely filled in with embroidery, pull the needle out of the piece through the same hole it originally went in, so that both yarn tails are coming out of the same hole. Tie a knot with both tails and hide them.

1

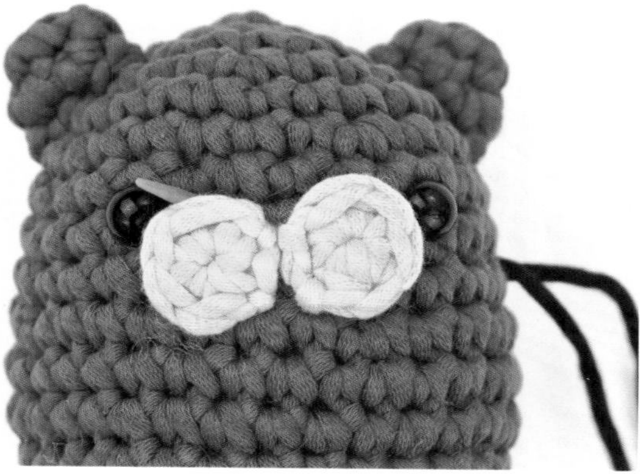

2

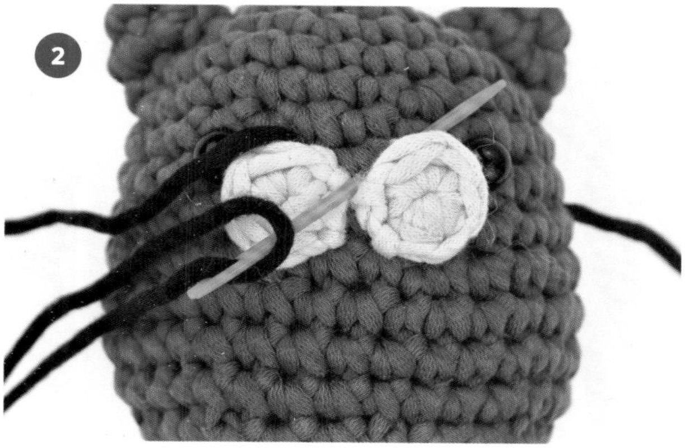

3

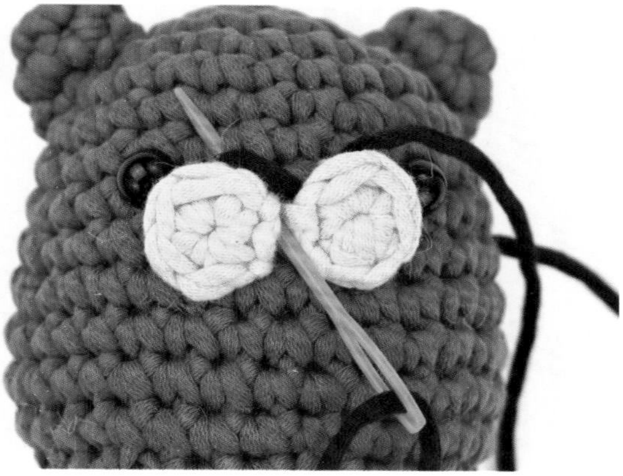

4

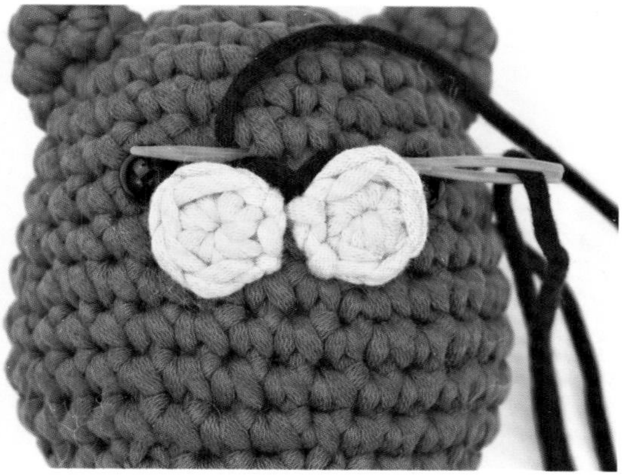

5

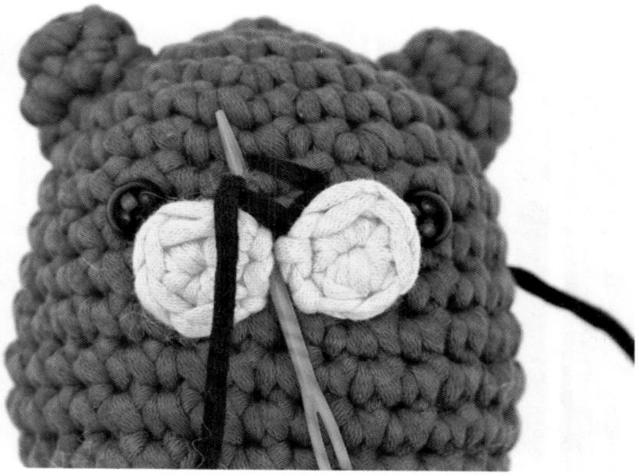

6

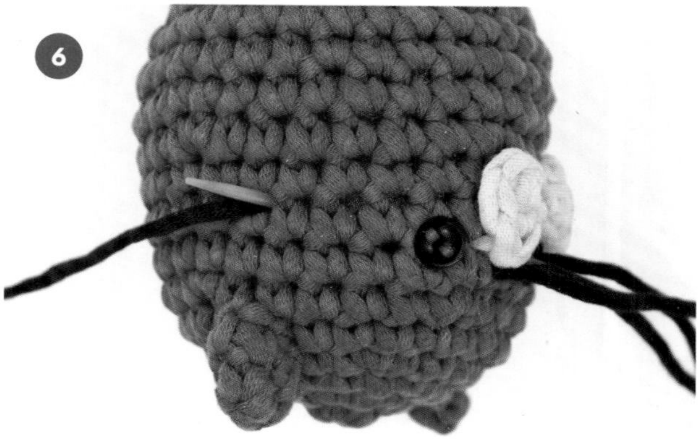

ARMS

With brown yarn (make four, two for each otter).

▶ Video tutorial at **thewoobles.com/celebrate**

Repeat the following steps four times to crochet four arms, one on each side of each otter:

Step 1.

Sl st join the yarn to one side of the body between rounds 10 and 11, two stitches away from the bottom of the snout. Insert the hook into the body from the back to the front of the body.

TIP Sl st join means slip stitch join. See tutorial on page 29.

Step 2.

Ch 3.

TIP When crocheting a new row, remember to skip the first stitch from the hook. And for the first row after a chain, remember to crochet under the back loops only. See tutorial on page 47.

Step 3.

2 sc.

Step 4.

Sl st in the stitch where you made the sl st join, from the front to the back of the body. Both yarn tails should be coming out of the same hole.

Step 5.

Fasten off. Tie both yarn tails together and hide them.

TOP HAT

With black and white yarn.

Rnd 1.   (black yarn) start 6 sc in magic loop (6)
Rnd 2.   6 inc (12)
Rnd 3.   [sc, inc] x 6 (18)
Rnd 4.   18 sc blo (18)

> **TIP** blo means to do the stitch through the back loop only. See page 23 for a picture of a back loop.

Rnds 5–7.   18 sc (18)
Rnd 8.   [inc flo, 2 sc flo] x 6 (24)

> **TIP** flo means to do the stitch through the front loop only. See page 23 for a picture of a front loop.

Rnd 9.   [3 sc, inc] x 6 (30)

Invisible fasten off leaving a long tail. Leave this yarn tail for now; you'll use it later.

Add a white band around the base of the hat:

Step 1.
Thread a needle with an arm's length of white yarn. Working on the inside of the hat, insert the needle through to the outside, in the round where the bottom of the hat and the rim meet. Leave a 6-inch tail.

Step 2.
Wrap the yarn twice around the base of the hat. Insert the needle back through the same hole it originally came out from, from the outside back to the inside of the hat.

Step 3.
Tie a knot with both of the white yarn tails and weave in ends.

Optionally stuff the hat. Thread a needle with the black yarn tail. Use it to sew the hat to the top of one otter. Hide the yarn tail.

LEAVES

With green yarn.

Row 1.   ch 7 (7)

TIP When crocheting a new row, remember to skip the first stitch from the hook. And for the first row after a chain, remember to crochet under the back loops only. See tutorial on page 47.

Row 2.   sl st, sc, hdc, dc, hdc, sl st, ch 7 (13)

TIP Hdc means half double crochet; see tutorial on page 34. Dc means double crochet; see tutorial on page 35.

Row 3.   sl st, sc, hdc, dc, hdc, sl st (6)

Fasten off leaving a long tail. Thread a needle with the tail. Use it to sew the two leaves in front of one of the ears on the second otter, at a 45-degree angle.

FLOWERS

With white and pink yarn (make one in each color).

Row 1.   ch 7 (7)

TIP When crocheting a new row, remember to skip the first stitch from the hook. And for the first row after a chain, remember to crochet under the back loops only. See tutorial on page 47.

Row 2.   2 sc, [2 hdc in same st] x 2, [3 dc in same st] x 2 (12)

Fasten off leaving a long tail. Now turn this strip of yarn into a flower bud:

Step 1.
Roll up the strip into a flower bud, starting on the side without the yarn tails.

Step 2.
Thread a needle with the pink yarn tail. Use it to secure the flower bud's shape. Insert the needle through all of the flower layers and repeat one stitch over.

Step 3.
Repeat step 2 as many times as needed until the flower bud feels secure. When you're done, pull the needle out of the bottom of the flower.

Step 4.
Use the same needle and pink yarn tail to sew both flowers to the second otter, centering them on top of the leaves by its ear.

1

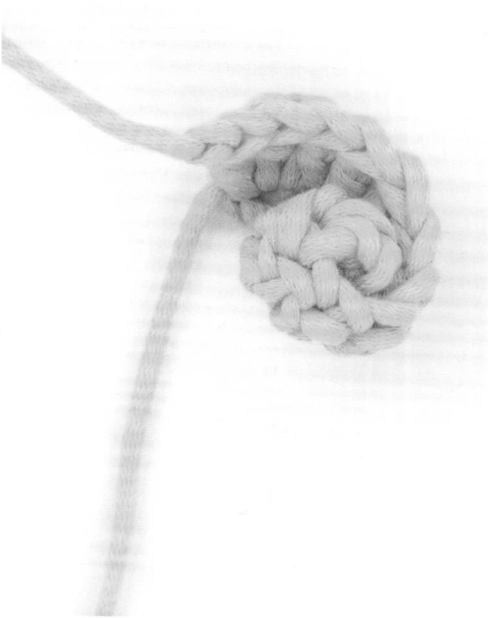

2

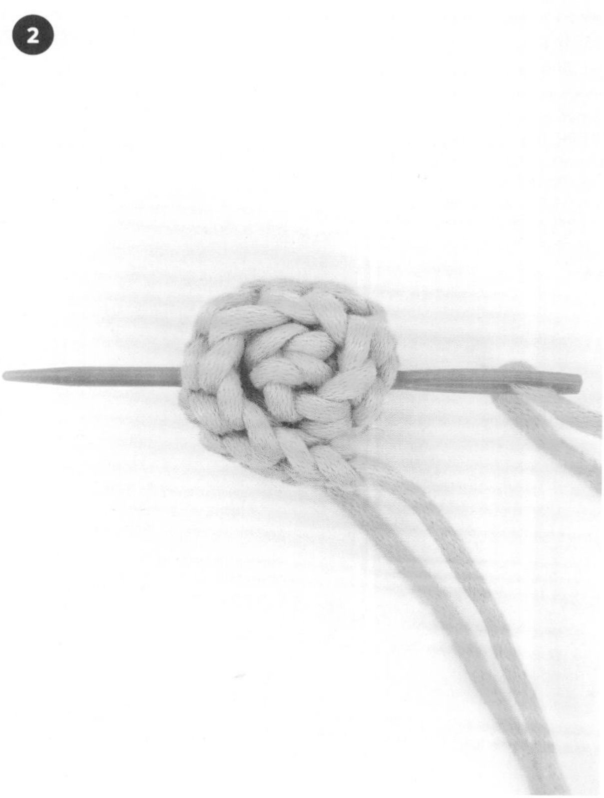

3

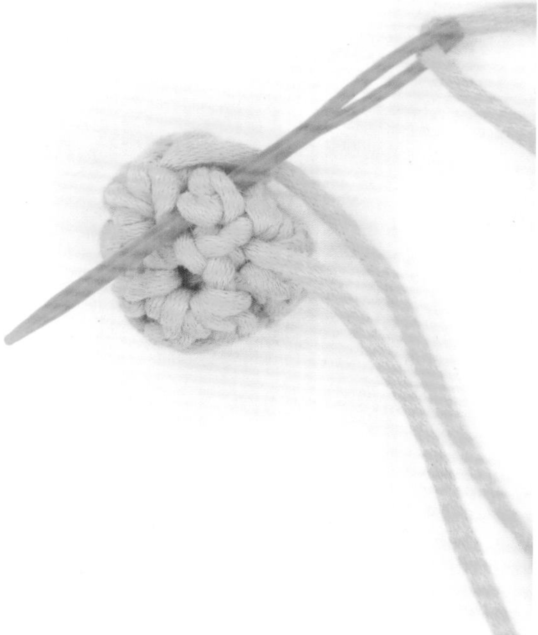

4

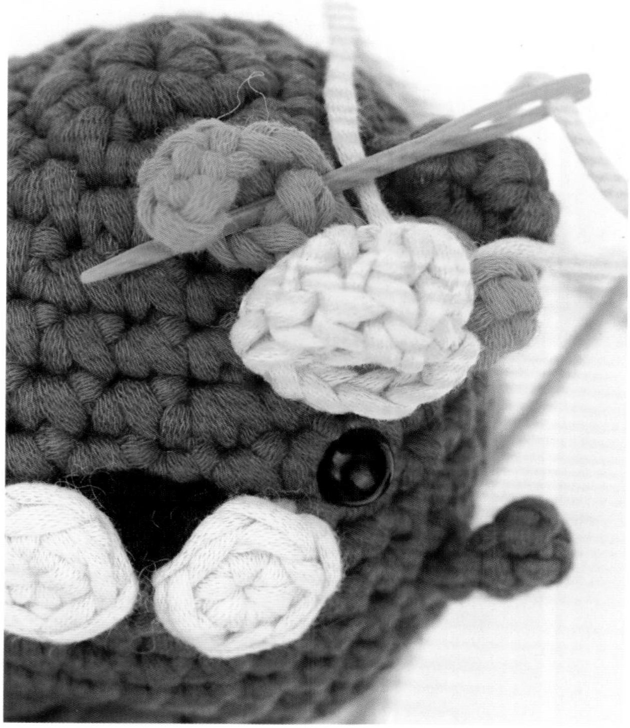

FINAL SIZE

Height: 4.5 in / 11.4 cm
Width: 3 in / 7.6 cm

YARN

The Woobles Easy Peasy Yarn
or any medium-weight #4 yarn
Yellow: What's Up Buttercup,
40 yds / 36 m
Black: The Coal Shebang,
15 yds / 14 m
White: Snow Place Like Home,
6 yds / 6 m

CROCHET HOOK

US G-6 / 4mm

OTHER MATERIALS

- One pair of 10mm black safety eyes
- Stuffing
- Stitch marker
- Tapestry needle

VIDEOS

 thewoobles.com/celebrate

CORNELIUS THE BEE

The Perfect Bay-bee for Buzzy Lil' Fingers

Prepare to be bee-witched by the un-bee-lievably adorable Cornelius the Bee. Little ones won't be able to help pollen in love with this honey of a guy—who'll keep any bay-bee buzzy with his fun antennae, sweet wings, and bold stripes. So hooray for Cornelius, a cuddle-buddy who definitely lives up to the buzz!

HEAD AND BODY

With yellow and black yarn.

TIP Keep track of where you are by placing a stitch marker in the first stitch of the current round. See tutorial on page 24.

Rnd 1.	(yellow yarn) start 6 sc in magic loop (6)
Rnd 2.	6 inc (12)
Rnd 3.	[sc, inc] x 6 (18)
Rnd 4.	[inc, 2 sc] x 6 (24)
Rnd 5.	24 sc (24)
Rnd 6.	[5 sc, inc] x 4 (28)
Rnds 7-9.	28 sc (28)

TIP Since we're making stripes that go all around the bee, instead of crocheting over the yellow yarn in the upcoming color change, you can leave it where it is for a neater look. When you switch back to yellow yarn, it'll be right there for you to pick up again. Remember to switch colors in the last step of the stitch before the color change. See color change tutorial on page 50.

Rnd 10.	(switch to black yarn) [6 sc, inc] x 4 (32)
Rnd 11.	32 sc (32)
Rnds 12-13.	(switch to yellow yarn) 32 sc (32)
Rnd 14.	(switch to black yarn) [2 sc, dec] x 8 (24)
Rnd 15.	24 sc (24)
Rnd 16.	(switch to yellow yarn) [sc, dec] x 8 (16)
Rnd 17.	16 sc (16)

Cut the black yarn.

Attach the eyes between rounds 7 and 8, with a 6-stitch space between them. If this amigurumi is for a baby or pet, embroider the eyes instead (see tutorial on page 56). Stuff the piece, shaping it like an egg.

Rnd 18.   8 dec (8)

Fasten off leaving a long tail. Thread a needle with the yarn tail. Use it to pull the yarn tail through the front loops of each stitch. Pull tight to close the remaining gap.

WINGS

With white yarn (make two).

Rnd 1.   start 6 sc in magic loop (6)
Rnd 2.   2 hdc in each stitch (12)

TIP Hdc means half double crochet. See tutorial on page 34.

Invisible fasten off leaving a long tail. Thread a needle with the tail. Use it to sew the wings vertically to the back of the bee's body, above the top black stripe, leaving a 4-stitch space between them. Make sure the "right side" of each wing faces out so the wings curve correctly.

TIP There's a so-called "right" and "wrong" side of crochet. See picture on page 22.

ANTENNAE

With black yarn (make two).

Crochet and secure the antennae on top of the bee's head:

Step 1.
Cut a forearm's length of yarn. Insert the hook between rounds 2 and 3, in the middle of the body, and pull one end of the yarn through.

Step 2.
Secure the antenna to the head by knotting the two yarn tails together as close to the head as possible.

Step 3.
Tie a knot in one of the yarn tails about an inch from the bee's head. Trim the yarn tail as close as possible to this knot.

Step 4.
Hide the other yarn tail in the head. Pull the yarn tail through the body in the opposite direction as the antenna to create tension to help the antenna stand upright.

SMILE

With black yarn.

Thread a needle with a forearm's length of yarn. Use it to embroider a smile, centered between the eyes, on round 8. The smile should be one round tall and two stitches wide.

TIP See tutorial for embroidering a curve on page 58.

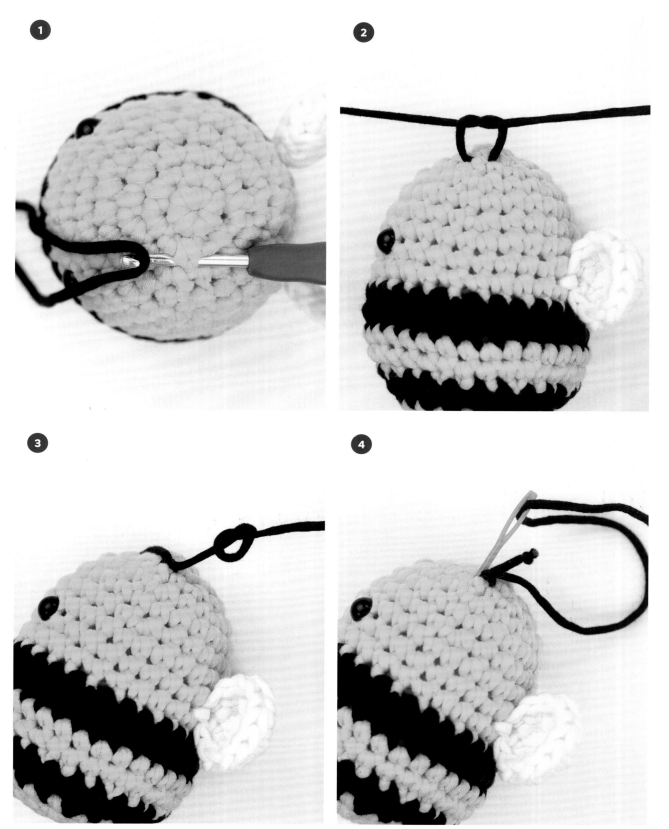

HUBERT THE FROG
100% Guarantee for a Hoppy Baby Shower

FINAL SIZE

Height: 3.5 in / 8.9 cm

Width: 4 in / 10.2 cm

YARN

The Woobles Easy Peasy Yarn

or any medium-weight #4 yarn

Green: Leaf It to Us, 20 yds / 18 m

Black: The Coal Shebang,
2 yds / 1.8 m

CROCHET HOOK

US G-6 / 4mm

OTHER MATERIALS

 Stuffing

 Stitch marker

 Tapestry needle

VIDEOS

▶ thewoobles.com/celebrate

Allow us to introduce Hubert the Frog, who is so very hoppy to meet you! This easy-to-grab ring is toad-ally great for keeping curious little fingers busy. And with his cute smile and friendly eyeballs, he's the perfect partner to help any tadpole shake, rattle, and roll their way to a hoppin' good time!

RING

With green yarn.

TIP Keep track of where you are by placing a stitch marker in the first stitch of the current round. See page 24 for a tutorial.

Rnd 1.   ch 25. Bend the chain into a U, being careful not to twist it, and sl st in the front loop of the first stitch. (25)

Rnd 2.	25 sc (25)
Rnd 3.	[4 sc, inc] x 5 (30)
Rnd 4.	[inc, 5 sc] x 5 (35)
Rnds 5-6.	35 sc (35)
Rnd 7.	[dec, 5 sc] x 5 (30)
Rnd 8.	[4 sc, dec] x 5 (25)

Invisible fasten off leaving a long tail. Flatten the ring and line up both edges. Thread a needle with the tail. Use it to whip stitch the two edges together, lightly stuffing along the way.

TIP See whip stitch tutorial on page 68.

EYES

With green and black yarn (make two).

Rnd 1.	(green yarn) start 6 sc in magic loop (6)
Rnd 2.	[sc, inc] x 3 (9)
Rnd 3.	9 sc (9)

Invisible fasten off leaving a long tail. Thread a needle with the tail. Use it to sew the eye bump to the outer edge of the ring, leaving a 4-stitch space between them.

Thread a needle with an arm's length of black yarn. Use it to embroider an eye in the center of each green eye bump.

TIP See tutorial for embroidering an eye on page 56.

SMILE

With black yarn.

Thread a needle with a forearm's length of yarn. Use it to embroider a smile in the middle of the ring, centered between the eyes. The smile should be one round tall and three stitches wide.

TIP See tutorial for embroidering a curve on page 58.

FINAL SIZE

Height: 4 in / 10.2 cm
Width: 5 in / 12.7 cm

YARN

The Woobles Easy Peasy Yarn
or any medium-weight #4 yarn
White: Snow Place Like Home,
40 yds / 36 m
Black: The Coal Shebang,
10 yds / 9 m
Blue: Seas the Day, 8 yds / 7 m
Orange: Orange You Glad,
1 yd / 1 m

CROCHET HOOK

US G-6 / 4mm

OTHER MATERIALS

◎◎ One pair of 10mm black
    safety eyes
◯ Stuffing
◯ Stitch marker
✎ Tapestry needle

VIDEOS

▶ thewoobles.com/celebrate

URKEL PHILIBERT THE STORK

Totally Storked for Your Special Delivery

For those super special deliveries, you'll have no egrets with Urkel Philibert the Stork. Swift and steady, he'll make sure your precious bundle arrives right on time for the happiest bird-day ever. And before you know it, you'll be busy playing beak-a-boo with that adorable little chirp off the old block!

HEAD AND BODY

With white yarn.

> **TIP** Keep track of where you are by placing a stitch marker in the first stitch of the current round. See page 24 for a tutorial.

Rnd 1.	start 6 sc in magic loop (6)
Rnd 2.	6 inc (12)
Rnd 3.	[sc, inc] x 6 (18)
Rnd 4.	[inc, 2 sc] x 6 (24)
Rnd 5.	24 sc (24)
Rnd 6.	[5 sc, inc] x 4 (28)
Rnds 7-9.	28 sc (28)
Rnd 10.	[6 sc, inc] x 4 (32)
Rnds 11-13.	32 sc (32)
Rnd 14.	[2 sc, dec] x 8 (24)
Rnd 15.	24 sc (24)
Rnd 16.	[sc, dec] x 8 (16)
Rnd 17.	16 sc (16)

Attach the eyes between rounds 7 and 8, with a 6-stitch space between them. If this amigurumi is for a baby or pet, embroider the eyes instead (see tutorial on page 56). Stuff the piece, shaping it like an egg.

Rnd 18.	8 dec (8)

Fasten off leaving a long tail. Thread a needle with the tail. Use it to pull the yarn tail through the front loops of each stitch. Pull tight to close the remaining gap.

BEAK

With orange yarn.

Rnd 1.   start 3 sc in magic loop (3)
Rnd 2.   3 inc (6)
Rnds 3–4.   6 sc (6)

Fasten off leaving a 6-inch tail and flatten the beak. Thread a needle with the yarn tail. Use it to sew the beak to the body just below and centered between the eyes, at round 9.

WINGS

With white and black yarn (make two).

Rnd 1.   (black yarn) start 4 sc in magic loop (4)
Rnd 2.   4 inc (8)

TIP You're changing colors in the next round. Remember to switch colors in the last step of the stitch before the color change. See tutorial on page 50.

Rnd 3.   (switch to white yarn) 8 sc, ch 1 (8)

Cut the black yarn.

Single crochet the two sides of the open edge of each wing together:

Step 1.
Flatten the wing and insert the hook under the first two stiches across from each other. Sc.

Step 2.
Continue to sc together the next three pairs of stitches. Fasten off leaving a long tail.

Thread a needle with the tail. Use it to sew the wings to either side of the stork two stitches back from the eyes, between rounds 10 and 11.

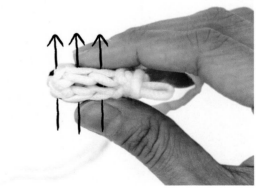

TAIL

With black yarn.

Crochet a four-feathered tail and sew it onto the stork's body:

Step 1.
Ch 8. Mark the first chain with a stitch marker.

Step 2.
Fold the chain in half and sl st into the front loop of the chain marked by the stitch marker.

Step 3.
[Ch 8, sl st into the chain marked by the stitch marker] x 3.

Step 4.
Fasten off leaving a long yarn tail. Thread a needle with the yarn tail. Use it to sew the stork's tail piece to the center lower back of the body, between rounds 14 and 15.

BUNDLE

With blue yarn.

Rnd 1.	start 6 sc in magic loop (6)
Rnd 2.	6 inc (12)
Rnd 3.	12 sc (12)
Rnd 4.	[sc, inc] x 6 (18)
Rnd 5.	18 sc (18)
Rnd 6.	[dec, sc] x 6 (12)
Rnd 7.	6 dec (6)

Stuff the piece.

Rnd 8.   For round 8, you'll make the ends of the stork's bundle:

▶ Video tutorial at **thewoobles.com/celebrate**

Step 1.
Sl st, ch 4.

> **TIP** When crocheting into a chain, crochet the first sc in the second chain from the hook.

Step 2.
In the chain you just made, 2 sc, sl st.

Step 3.
Along the bundle's rim, 2 sc.

Step 4.
Repeat steps 1-3.

Rnd 9.	sc, ch 1 and turn (2)
Rnd 10.	2 sc (2)

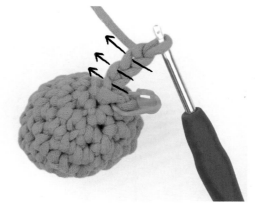

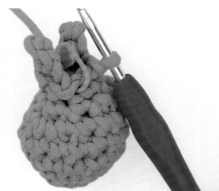

Fasten off leaving a long tail. Thread a needle with the tail. Use it to sew the bundle's opening shut by whip stitching the flap to the other side of the opening.

TIP See whip stitch tutorial on page 68.

Optionally sew the bundle to the bottom of the beak.

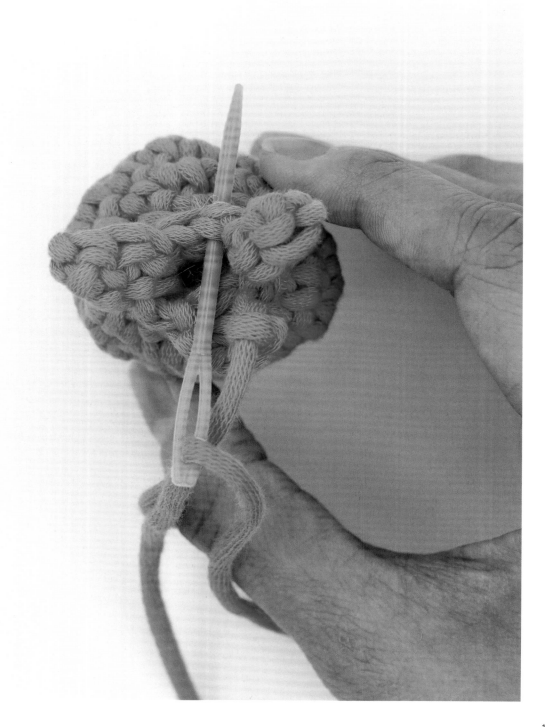

OUTER SPACE MOBILE

A Mobile That's Out of This World

This adorable mobile will spin its way right into your heart. Parents will be over the moon when Stella the Astronaut and those space-tastic stars and planets help their babies blast off toward naptime! Whether they're exploring their fingers, toes, or the uncharted expanses of dreamland, this mobile is sure to rock-et their world. After making all four patterns, tie them onto your favorite baby mobile.

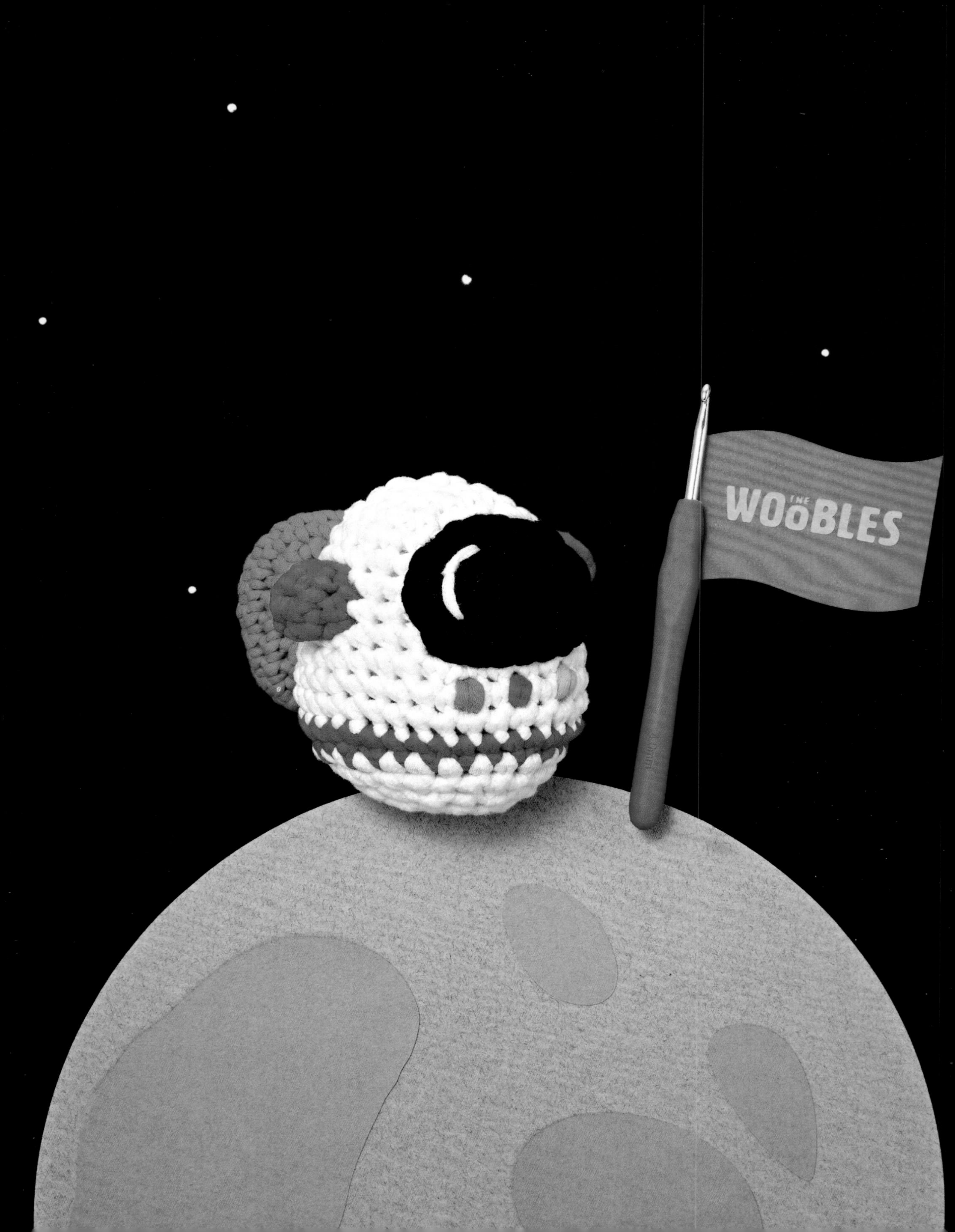
THE
WOOBLES

FINAL SIZE

Height: 3.5 in / 8.9 cm
Width: 2.5 in / 6.4 cm

YARN

The Woobles Easy Peasy Yarn

or any medium-weight #4 yarn

White: Snow Place Like Home,
40 yds / 36 m

Blue: Seas the Day, 10 yds / 9 m

Red: Let's Ketchup Soon,
7 yds / 6 m

Black: The Coal Shebang,
7 yd / 6 m

Yellow: What's Up Buttercup,
1 yd / 1 m

CROCHET HOOK

US G-6 / 4mm

OTHER MATERIALS

 Stuffing

 Stitch marker

 Tapestry needle

VIDEOS

(▷) thewoobles.com/celebrate

STELLA THE ASTRONAUT

HEAD AND BODY

With white and red yarn.

> **TIP** Keep track of where you are by placing a stitch marker in the first stitch of the current round. See tutorial on page 24.

Rnd 1.	(white yarn) start 6 sc in magic loop (6)
Rnd 2.	6 inc (12)
Rnd 3.	[sc, inc] x 6 (18)
Rnd 4.	[inc, 2 sc] x 6 (24)
Rnd 5.	24 sc (24)
Rnd 6.	[5 sc, inc] x 4 (28)
Rnds 7–9.	28 sc (28)
Rnd 10.	[6 sc, inc] x 4 (32)
Rnds 11–12.	32 sc (32)

> **TIP** Since we're making a stripe that goes all around the astronaut, instead of crocheting over the white yarn in the upcoming color change, you can leave it where it is for a neater look. When you switch back to white yarn, it'll be right there for you to pick up again. Remember to switch colors in the last step of the stitch before the color change. See color change tutorial on page 50.

Rnd 13.	(switch to red yarn) 32 sc (32)
Rnd 14.	(switch to white yarn) [2 sc, dec] x 8 (24)

Cut the red yarn.

Rnd 15.	24 sc (24)
Rnd 16.	[sc, dec] x 8 (16)
Rnd 17.	16 sc (16)

Stuff the piece, shaping it like an egg.

Rnd 18.	8 dec (8)

Fasten off leaving a long tail. Thread a needle with the tail. Use it to pull the yarn tail through the front loops of each stitch. Pull tight to close the remaining gap.

FACE

With black and white yarn.

TIP This is an oval. See tutorial on page 48.

Rnd 1. (black yarn) ch 6 (6)
Rnd 2. 4 sc, then 3 sc in the last st. Rotate the piece to work on the opposite side of the foundation chain. 3 sc, inc, sl st into the first sc of round 2 (12)
Rnd 3. [3 sc, 3 inc] x 2 (18)
Rnd 4. 3 sc, [sc, inc] x 3, 3 sc, [sc, inc] x 3 (24)

Invisible fasten off leaving a long tail. Thread a needle with the tail. Use it to sew the face onto the body, opposite the zigzag from the color change, spanning rounds 4 to 9.

For the shine of the helmet, thread a needle with an arm's length of white yarn. Use it to embroider a curve along the top left edge of the face.

TIP See tutorial for embroidering a curve on page 58.

BACKPACK

With blue yarn.

Rnd 1. start 4 sc in magic loop (4)
Rnd 2. [3 sc in same st] x 4 (12)
Rnd 3. sc, [(3 sc in same st), 2 sc] x 3, 3 sc in same st, sc (20)
Rnd 4. 2 sc, [(3 sc in same st), 4 sc] x 3, 3 sc in same st, 2 sc (28)
Rnds 5–7. 28 sc (28)
Rnd 8. 2 sc, sc3tog, [4sc, sc3tog] x 3, 2 sc (20)

TIP Sc3tog means single crochet 3 stitches together. See tutorial on page 38.

Stuff the piece.

Rnd 9. [2 sc, sc3tog] x 4 (12)
Rnd 10. sc3tog x 4 (4)

Fasten off leaving a long tail. Thread a needle with the tail. Use it to pull the yarn tail through the front loops of each stitch. Pull tight to close the remaining gap. Sew the backpack to the middle back of the astronaut. The bottom of the backpack should line up with the bottom of the red stripe on the astronaut's body.

EARS

With red yarn (make two).

Rnd 1.   start 8 sc in magic loop (8)
Rnd 2.   8 sc (8)

Invisible fasten off leaving a long tail. Thread a needle with the tail. Use it to sew on both ears, one on either side of the astronaut's head, spanning rounds 6 to 8.

BUTTONS

With blue, red, and yellow yarn.

Thread a needle with an arm's length of yarn. Use it to embroider one button in each color between the face and the red stripe, leaving two stitches between buttons, spanning round 11.

TIP Use the same technique for the buttons that you use to embroider eyes (see tutorial on page 56).

PLANET

FINAL SIZE

Height: 4 in / 10.2 cm

Width: 4 in / 10.2 cm

YARN

The Woobles Easy Peasy Yarn

or any medium-weight #4 yarn

Orange: Orange You Glad,
40 yds / 36 m

Yellow: What's Up Buttercup,
20 yds / 18 m

Blue: Seas the Day, 2 yds / 2 m

CROCHET HOOK

US G-6 / 4mm

OTHER MATERIALS

⊙⊙ One pair of 10mm black
safety eyes

☁ Stuffing

◠ Stitch marker

✎ Tapestry needle

VIDEOS

▶ thewoobles.com/celebrate

BODY

With orange yarn.

> **TIP** Keep track of where you are by placing stitch marker in first stitch of current round. See tutorial on page 24.

Rnd 1.   start 6 sc in magic loop (6)

Rnd 2.   6 inc (12)

Rnd 3.   [sc, inc] x 6 (18)

Rnd 4.   [inc, 2 sc] x 6 (24)

Rnd 5.   [3 sc, inc] x 6 (30)

Rnd 6.   [inc, 4 sc] x 6 (36)

Rnds 7-8.   36 sc (36)

Rnds 9-10.   36 sc blo (36)

> **TIP** blo means to do the stitch through the back loop only. See page 23 for a picture of a back loop.

Rnds 11-12.   36 sc (36)

Rnd 13.   [dec, 4 sc] x 6 (30)

Rnd 14.   [3 sc, dec] x 6 (24)

Rnd 15.   [dec, 2 sc] x 6 (18)

Attach the eyes between rounds 12 and 13, with a 7-stitch space between them. If this amigurumi is for a baby or pet, embroider the eyes instead (see tutorial on page 56). Stuff the piece.

Rnd 16.   [sc, dec] x 6 (12)

Rnd 17.   6 dec (6)

Fasten off leaving a long tail. Thread a needle with the tail. Use it to pull the yarn tail through the front loops of each stitch. Pull tight to close the remaining gap and hide the tail.

RING

With yellow and blue yarn.

Crochet a ring directly onto the body of the planet:

Step 1.
(yellow yarn) Sl st join the yarn in the last unworked front loop from round 10 of the body.

> **TIP** Sl st join means slip stitch join. See tutorial on page 69. See a picture of a front loop on page 23.

Step 2.
Ch 3, dc in the same stitch as the sl st join.

> **TIP** Dc means double crochet; see tutorial on page 35.

Step 3.
Dc in each available front loop, making a yellow ring around the body. Fasten off and hide the yarn tail.

Step 4.
(blue yarn) Sl st join the blue yarn to the yellow ring, in the back loop of the first dc and the front loop of the dc immediately above it.

> **TIP** If this step is confusing, think of it this way: You're using the blue yarn to sl st join two yellow rounds together.

Step 5.
Sl st through the back loop of the bottom stitch and front loop of the top stitch all the way around.

Step 6.
To finish, sl st into first sl st to create one continuous ring. Fasten off and hide the yarn tail.

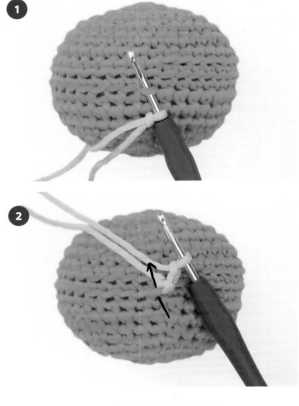

ROCKET

FINAL SIZE

Height: 4 in / 10.2 cm
Width: 4 in / 10.2 cm

YARN

The Woobles Easy Peasy Yarn
or any medium-weight #4 yarn
Blue: Seas the Day, 40 yds / 36 m
Red: Let's Ketchup Soon,
20 yds / 18 m
Yellow: What's Up Buttercup,
1 yd / 1 m

CROCHET HOOK

US G-6 / 4mm

OTHER MATERIALS

- Stuffing
- Stitch marker
- Tapestry needle

VIDEOS

 thewoobles.com/celebrate

BODY

With red and blue yarn.

TIP Keep track of where you are by placing a stitch marker in the first stitch of the current round. See tutorial on page 24.

Rnd 1.   (red yarn) start 6 sc in magic loop (6)
Rnd 2.   6 inc (12)
Rnd 3.   [sc, inc] x 6 (18)
Rnd 4.   [inc, 2 sc] x 6 (24)
Rnd 5.   24 sc (24)

TIP You're changing colors in the next round. Remember to switch colors in the last step of the stitch before the color change. See tutorial on page 50.

Rnd 6.   (switch to blue yarn) [5 sc, inc] x 4 (28)

Cut the red yarn.

Rnds 7–9.   28 sc (28)
Rnd 10.   [6 sc, inc] x 4 (32)
Rnds 11–13. 32 sc (32)
Rnd 14.   [2 sc, dec] x 8 (24)
Rnd 15.   24 sc (24)
Rnd 16.   [sc, dec] x 8 (16)
Rnd 17.   16 sc (16)

Stuff the piece, shaping it like an egg.

Rnd 18.   8 dec (8)

Fasten off leaving a long tail. Thread a needle with the tail. Use it to pull the yarn tail through the front loops of each stitch. Pull tight to close the remaining gap.

WINDOW

With yellow yarn.

Rnd 1.   start 6 sc in magic loop (6)
Rnd 2.   6 inc (12)

Invisible fasten off leaving a long tail. Thread a needle with the tail. Use it to sew the window to the front of the rocket, spanning rounds 9 to 12.

FINS

With red yarn (make two).

Rnd 1.   start 3 sc in magic loop (3)
Rnd 2.   sc, [2 hdc in same st], sc (4)

TIP Hdc means half double crochet. See tutorial on page 34.

Rnd 3.   sc, [2 dc in same st] x 2, sc (6)

TIP Dc means double crochet. See tutorial on page 35.

Rnd 4.   2 sc, [2 hdc in same st] x 2, 2 sc (8)

Invisible fasten off leaving a long tail. Thread a needle with the tail. Use it to sew the fins to either side of the rocket, spanning rounds 11 to 14.

THRUSTER

With red yarn.

Rnd 1.   ch 16, sl st in the first stitch of this round. Be careful not to twist the chain. (16)

TIP When crocheting into a chain, remember to crochet only into the back loops. See a picture of back loops on page 23.

Rnd 2.   16 sc (16)

Invisible fasten off leaving a long tail. Thread a needle with the tail. Use it to sew the ring to the bottom of the rocket, between rounds 16 and 17.

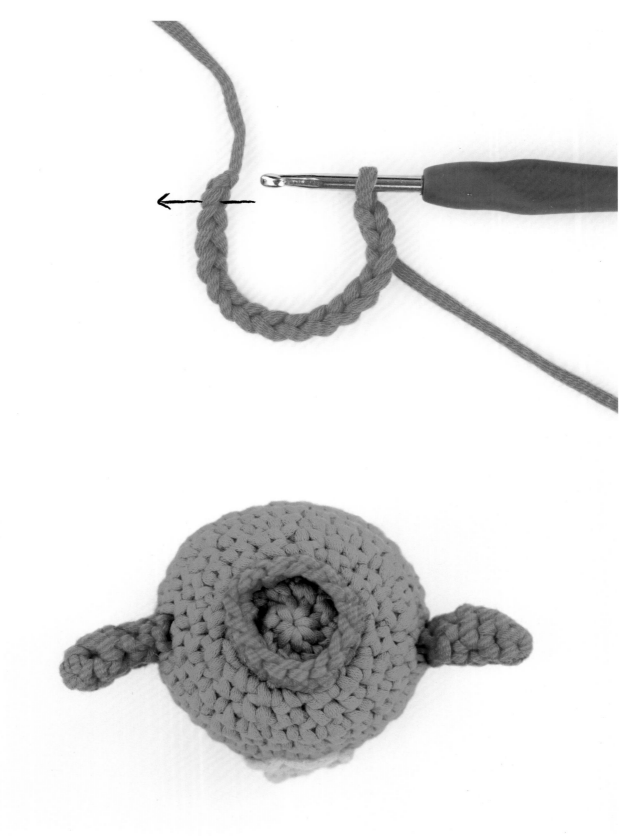

STAR

FINAL SIZE

Height: 3.5 in. / 8.9 cm
Width: 3 in. / 7.6 cm

YARN

The Woobles Easy Peasy Yarn
or any medium-weight #4 yarn
Yellow: What's Up Buttercup,
30 yds / 27 m

CROCHET HOOK

US G-6 / 4mm

OTHER MATERIALS

- One pair of 10mm black safety eyes
- Stuffing
- Stitch marker
- Tapestry needle

VIDEOS

 thewoobles.com/celebrate

BODY

With yellow yarn (make two).

TIP Keep track of where you are by placing a stitch marker in the first stitch of the current round. See tutorial on page 24.

Rnd 1.   start 5 sc in magic loop (5)
Rnd 2.   5 inc (10)
Rnd 3.   [sc, inc] x 5 (15)
Rnd 4.   [inc, 2 sc] x 5 (20)
Rnd 5.   [(in same st: hdc, dc, hdc, sc), 3 sl st] x 5 (35)

TIP Hdc means half double crochet. See tutorial on page 34. Dc means double crochet. See tutorial on page 35.

Rnd 6.   [sc, hdc, 3 dc in same st, hdc, sc, 2 sl st] x 5 (45)

For the first star (front), fasten off and weave in the yarn tail on the "wrong" side of the piece.

TIP There's a so-called "right" and "wrong" side of crochet. See picture on page 22.

Attach the eyes between rounds 3 and 4 on the "right side" of the piece, with a 5-stitch space between them. If this amigurumi is for a baby or pet, embroider the eyes instead (see tutorial on page 56).

For the second star (back), fasten off leaving a long tail. Put the "wrong" sides of the two stars back-to-back, with the eyes facing out. Thread a needle with the tail. Use it to whip stitch the back loops of one piece to the front loops of the other piece to close it. Stuff as you go.

TIP See whip stitch tutorial on page 68. See page 23 for a picture of a back loop. See page 23 for a picture of a front loop.

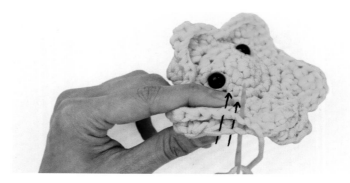

FINAL SIZE

Height: 18 in / 45.7 cm
Width: 14 in / 35.6 cm

YARN

The Woobles Easy Peasy Yarn
or any medium-weight #4 yarn

White: Snow Place Like Home,
283 yds / 259 m

Tan: This Sand is Your Sand,
40 yds / 36 m

Black: The Coal Shebang,
1 yd / 1 m

CROCHET HOOK

US G-6 / 4mm

OTHER MATERIALS

 Stuffing
 Stitch marker
 Tapestry needle

VIDEOS

 thewoobles.com/celebrate

OLLIE THE LAMB
Snuggle Ewe and Your Baa-by

Hey, have you herd? Ollie the Lamb is here to keep your baa-by warm and snuggly with this cozy lovey blanket. Not only is it woolly, woolly soft, but it's also the perfect reminder of how much ewe love them. And with Ollie's fluffy head and sweet little hooves, he's maybe the cutest nap partner ever.

BODY

With white yarn.

Row 1.   ch 42 (42)

TIP When crocheting a new row, remember to skip the first stitch from the hook. And for the first row after a chain, remember to crochet under the back loops only. See tutorial on page 47.

Rows 2-4.   41 sc, ch 1 and turn (41)
Row 5.   sc, [sc, dc5tog] x 19, 2 sc, ch 1 and turn (41)

TIP Dc5tog means double crochet 5 stitches together. It's also called a bobble stitch. See tutorial on page 36.

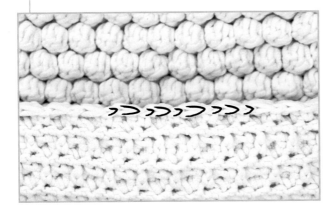

Row 6.	41 sc, ch 1 and turn (41)
Row 7.	2 sc, [sc, dc5tog] x 18, 3 sc, ch 1 and turn (41)
Row 8.	41 sc, ch 1 and turn (41)
Rows 9–40.	Repeat rows 5 to 8 eight more times.
Row 41.	sc, [sc, dc5tog] x 19, 2 sc, ch 1 and turn (41)
Rows 42–44.	Repeat row 8

HEAD

With tan and white yarn.

Rnd 1.	(tan yarn) start 6 sc in magic loop (6)
Rnd 2.	6 inc (12)
Rnd 3.	[sc, inc] x 6 (18)
Rnd 4.	[inc, 2 sc] x 6 (24)
Rnd 5.	24 sc (24)
Rnd 6.	[5 sc, inc] x 4 (28)
Rnds 7–9.	28 sc (28)
Rnd 10.	[6 sc, inc] x 4 (32)

Rnd 11.	(switch to white yarn) [dc5tog, sc] x 16 (32)
Rnd 12.	[6 sc, dec] x 4 (28)
Rnd 13.	[sc, dc5tog] x 14 (28)
Rnd 14.	[dec, 5 sc] x 4 (24)
Rnd 15.	[dc5tog, sc] x 12 (24)
Rnd 16.	[sc, dec] x 8 (16)
Rnd 17.	[sc, dc5tog] x 8 (16)

Stuff the piece, shaping it like an egg.

Rnd 18.	8 dec (8)

Fasten off leaving a long tail. Thread a needle with the tail. Use it to pull the yarn tail through the front loops of each stitch. Pull tight to close the remaining gap. Use the remaining yarn tail to sew the white end of the head to the middle of the first row of the body.

EARS

With tan yarn (make two).

Rnd 1.   start 6 sc in magic loop (6)
Rnd 2.   [sc, inc] x 3 (9)
Rnd 3.   [inc, 2 sc] x 3 (12)
Rnd 4.   [3 sc, inc] x 3 (15)
Rnd 5.   15 sc (15)
Rnd 6.   [dec, sc] x 5 (10)
Rnd 7.   10 sc (10)

Invisible fasten off leaving a long tail. Sew the ears to either side of the white end of the head:

Step 1.
Thread a needle with the tail. Use it to whip stitch the open end of each ear closed.

TIP See whip stitch tutorial on page 68.

Step 2.
Fold each ear in half lengthwise and sew the bases of the ears so that they stay folded.

Step 3.
Sew the ears onto either side of the head, with the fold facing the tan part of the head, between the second and third rounds of dc5tog stitches.

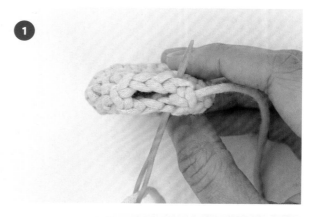

FACE

With black yarn.

To make the eyes, thread a needle with an arm's length of black yarn. Use it to embroider two curves roughly in line with the ears, spanning rounds 5 to 7.

TIP See tutorial for embroidering a curve on page 58.

Thread the needle with another arm's length of black yarn. Use it to embroider the nose and mouth:

Step 1.
Hold the head so the lamb's eyes are facing toward you. Insert the needle slightly up and to the right of the center of the magic loop, between rounds 2 and 3. Pull it out through the center, leaving a 6-inch tail.

Step 2.
Insert the needle in the same upper right-hand spot and pull it out the equivalent spot to the left of the center point.

Step 3.
Insert the needle in the center point and pull it out two rounds down.

Step 4.
Insert the needle in the center point. Pull the needle out where it originally went into the piece, so that both tails are coming out of the same hole. Tie a knot with both tails and hide them.

LEGS

With tan yarn (make four).

Rnd 1. start 6 sc in magic loop (6)
Rnd 2. 6 inc (12)
Rnds 3–5. 12 sc (12)
Rnd 6. [4 sc, dec] x 2 (10)
Rnds 7–8. 10 sc (10)

Lightly stuff all four legs, then invisible fasten off leaving a long tail. Flatten each leg and whip stitch the two sides of the open edge together. Sew one leg to each corner of the body.

TAIL

With white yarn.

Rnd 1. start 6 sc in magic loop (6)
Rnd 2. 6 inc (12)
Rnd 3. 12 sc (12)
Rnd 4. [sc, dec] x 4 (8)

Invisible fasten off leaving a long yarn tail. Flatten the lamb's tail piece and whip stitch the two sides of the open edge together. Sew the lamb tail to the middle of the last row of the body, opposite the head.

FINAL SIZE

Height: 1 in / 2.5 cm
Width: 7.5 in / 19.1 cm

YARN

The Woobles Easy Peasy Yarn
or any medium-weight #4 yarn
Yellow: What's Up Buttercup,
60 yds / 55 m
Orange: Orange You Glad,
1 yd / 1 m

CROCHET HOOK

US G-6 / 4mm

OTHER MATERIALS

 Stitch marker
 Tapestry needle

VIDEOS

thewoobles.com/celebrate

CAT TRAY

Litter-ally the Most Claw-some Tray ever

Don't settle for an in-fur-ior gift! This trinket tray is the purr-fect combo of cute and useful—just whisk-er all your coins and keys right into this paw-sitively delightful dish to keep them from getting lost. In fact, we're not kitten around when we say this is one gift you may just want to keep fur yourself!

TRAY

With yellow yarn.

> **TIP** Keep track of where you are by placing a stitch marker in the first stitch of the current round. See page 24 for a tutorial.

Rnd 1.	start 6 sc in magic loop (6)
Rnd 2.	6 inc (12)
Rnd 3.	[sc, inc] x 6 (18)
Rnd 4.	[inc, 2 sc] x 6 (24)
Rnd 5.	[3 sc, inc] x 6 (30)
Rnd 6.	[inc, 4 sc] x 6 (36)
Rnd 7.	[5 sc, inc] x 6 (42)
Rnd 8.	42 sc (42)

Invisible fasten off leaving a long tail. Let the "wrong side" face out.

> **TIP** There's a so-called "right" and "wrong" side of crochet. See picture on page 22.

EARS

With yellow yarn (make two).

Rnd 1.	start 3 sc in magic loop (3)
Rnd 2.	3 inc (6)

Invisible fasten off leaving a long tail. Thread a needle with the tail. Use it to sew the ears to the rim of the tray with a 5-stitch space between them.

TAIL

With yellow yarn.

Rnd 1.   start 4 sc in magic loop (4)

Rnd 2.   [sc, inc] x 2 (6)

Rnds 3–8. 6 sc (6)

Rnd 9.   [sc, dec] x 2 (4)

Invisible fasten off leaving a long yarn tail. Thread a needle with the yarn tail. Use it to sew the cat's tail piece opposite the ears on the "wrong side" of the tray, at round 7.

STRIPES

With orange yarn.

Embroider three stripes on the inside of the tray:

Step 1.
To begin the embroidery, thread a needle with an arm's length of yarn. Insert the needle from underneath the tray on the side closest to the ears, lined up with the left edge of the right ear between rounds 3 and 4. Leave a 6-inch tail.

Step 2.
To embroider the first stripe, insert the needle again four stitches to the left; then pull it out in the middle of the tray to define the start of the middle stripe, between rounds 3 and 4.

Step 3.
Embroider the middle stripe a little wider: Insert the needle five stitches to the right; then pull it out about two stitches away from the middle stripe to define the right edge of the third stripe.

Step 4.
To finish embroidering the third stripe, insert the needle four stitches to the left. Both yarn tails should now be on the underside of the tray.

Step 5.
Double knot both tails together as close as possible to where one of the tails exits the tray. Weave in both yarn tails.

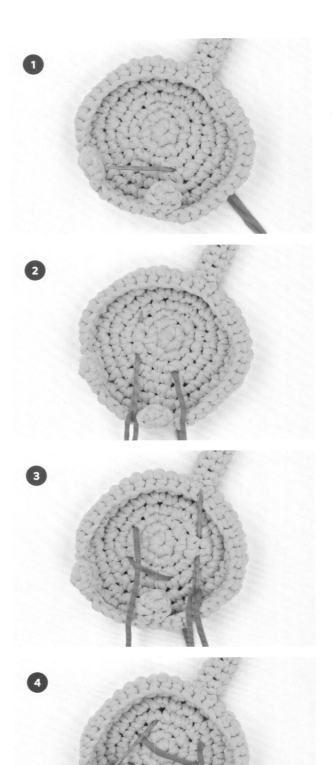

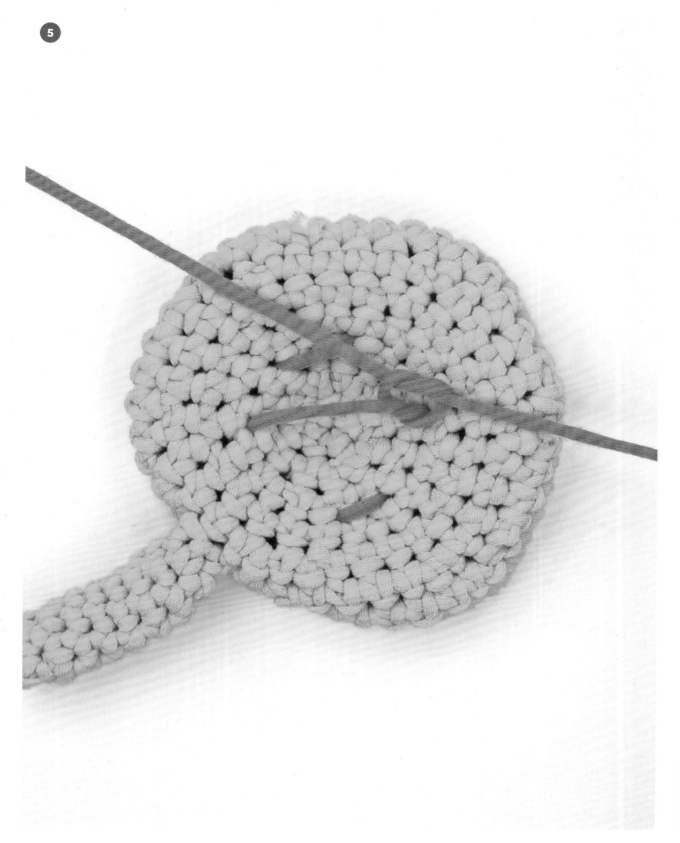

FINAL SIZE

Height: 4 in / 10.2 cm
Width: 5.5 in / 14 cm

YARN

The Woobles Easy Peasy Yarn
or any medium-weight #4 yarn
Green: Leaf It to Us, 50 yds / 46 m
Brown: A Whole Latte Love,
25 yds / 23 m
Pink: Eat, Pink & Be Merry,
2 yds / 2 m
Black: The Coal Shebang,
1 yd / 1 m

CROCHET HOOK

US G-6 / 4mm

OTHER MATERIALS

- One pair of 10mm black safety eyes
- Stuffing
- Stitch marker
- Tapestry needle

VIDEOS

 thewoobles.com/celebrate

CLINT THE CACTUS
To Sharpen Up Your New Digs

Our guy Clint is pretty fly for a cacti. He looks sharp but feels soft—perfect for sprucing up any shelf, table, or windowsill. Not only does he never need water, but he's always up for a cuddle, whether out of his cozy pot or in. Plus, that jaunty little flower is—not to put too fine a point on it—prickin' awesome.

HEAD AND BODY

With green yarn.

TIP Keep track of where you are by placing a stitch marker in the first stitch of current the round. See tutorial on page 24.

Rnd 1.	start 6 sc in magic loop (6)
Rnd 2.	6 inc (12)
Rnd 3.	[sc, inc] x 6 (18)
Rnd 4.	[inc, 2 sc] x 6 (24)
Rnd 5.	24 sc (24)
Rnd 6.	[5 sc, inc] x 4 (28)
Rnds 7-9.	28 sc (28)
Rnd 10.	[6 sc, inc] x 4 (32)
Rnds 11-13.	32 sc (32)
Rnd 14.	[2 sc, dec] x 8 (24)
Rnd 15.	24 sc (24)
Rnd 16.	[sc, dec] x 8 (16)
Rnd 17.	16 sc (16)

Attach the eyes between rounds 7 and 8, with a 6-stitch space between them. If this amigurumi is for a baby or pet, embroider the eyes instead (see tutorial on page 56). Stuff the piece, shaping it like an egg.

Rnd 18.	8 dec (8)

Fasten off leaving a long tail. Thread a needle with the tail. Use it to pull the yarn tail through the front loops of each stitch. Pull tight to close the remaining gap.

SMILE

With black yarn.

Thread a needle with a forearm's length of yarn. Use it to embroider a smile, centered between the eyes, on round 9. The smile should be one round tall and two stitches wide.

TIP See tutorial for embroidering a curve on page 58.

CACTUS DETAIL

With green yarn.

Embroider six evenly spaced vertical lines down the sides of the cactus to imitate the look of spiny ribs:

Step 1.
Thread a needle with at least one yard of yarn. Insert the needle through the center bottom of the cactus and up out the top. Leave a 6-inch tail.

Step 2.
To embroider the first line, draw the yarn down the body of the cactus between one eye and the nearest corner of the smile. Then insert the needle back through the center bottom of the cactus and out the top.

Step 3.
To embroider the second line, repeat step 2 between the other eye and other corner of the smile.

Step 4.
Continue the same way to embroider four more evenly spaced lines around the body of the cactus (from an overhead view, the lines should look like a six-sided asterisk).

Step 5.
When you've embroidered all six lines, bring the needle over one of the lines at the very top of the cactus. Then insert the needle through the top center of the cactus and out the bottom through the same hole it first came in, so that both yarn tails are coming out of the same hole. Tie a knot with both tails and hide them.

ARMS

With green yarn (make two).

Rnd 1.   start 4 sc in magic loop (4)
Rnd 2.   4 inc (8)
Rnds 3–4.   sc, 2 dc, sc, 4 sl st (8)

TIP Dc means double crochet. See tutorial on page 35.

Rnd 5.   8 sc (8)

Invisible fasten off leaving a long tail. Stuff lightly.

TIP Since the arms are so small, it can be easier to work with if you stuff them with scrap pieces of yarn instead of stuffing.

Thread a needle with the tail. Use it to sew the arms onto either side of the cactus body, spanning rounds 8 to 10. The arms should curve up.

FLOWER

With pink yarn.

Crochet a five-petal flower and sew it on top of the cactus:

Step 1.
Ch 5. Mark the first chain with a stitch marker.

Step 2.
Fold the chain in half and sl st into the chain marked by the stitch marker.

Step 3.
[Ch 4, sl st into the chain marked by the stitch marker] x 4.

Step 4.
Fasten off leaving a long tail. Thread a needle with the tail. Use it to sew the flower to the top of the cactus.

POT

With brown yarn.

Rnd 1.   start 6 sc in magic loop (6)
Rnd 2.   6 inc (12)
Rnd 3.   [sc, inc] x 6 (18)
Rnd 4.   [inc, 2 sc] x 6 (24)
Rnd 5.   [3 sc, inc] x 6 (30)
Rnd 6.   30 sc blo (30)

TIP blo means to do the stitch through the back loop only. See page 23 for a picture of a back loop.

Rnd 7.   [inc, 9 sc] x 3 (33)
Rnd 8.   33 sc (33)
Rnd 9.   [10 sc blo, inc blo] x 3 (36)
Rnd 10.   36 sc (36)
Rnd 11.   36 sc flo (36)

TIP flo means to do the stitch through the front loop only. See page 23 for a picture of a front loop.

Rnd 12.   36 sc (36)

Invisible fasten off leaving a long tail. Fold the top over at round 11. The edge should match up with the leftover front loops of round 9. Thread a needle with the tail. Use it to whip stitch the edge and the front loops of round 9 together. Weave in the yarn tails on the inside of the pot.

TIP See whip stitch tutorial on page 68.

MUSHROOM HOUSE

An A-spore-able Addition to Any Room

The perfect gift for that fun-gi, gal, or non-binary pal with a fabulous new address! This little house will fit into any nook or cranny, even if there isn't mush-room. Though with its whiff of woodland magic, it would work just as well in an enchanted forest. Either way, it's so cute that it'd be practically im-morel not to show it off.

LOWER BASE

With tan yarn.

> **TIP** Keep track of where you are by placing a stitch marker in the first stitch of the current round. See tutorial on page 24.

Rnd 1.	start 8 sc in magic loop	(8)
Rnd 2.	8 inc	(16)
Rnd 3.	16 sc	(16)
Rnd 4.	[sc, inc] x 8	(24)
Rnd 5.	24 sc	(24)
Rnd 6.	[inc, 2 sc] x 8	(32)
Rnds 7-9.	32 sc	(32)
Rnd 10.	[6 sc, dec] x 4	(28)
Rnds 11-13.	28 sc	(28)

Stuff the lower base. Invisible fasten off leaving a long tail and set it aside for now—you'll use it to sew the lower base to the upper base later.

FINAL SIZE
Height: 4.5 in / 11.4 cm
Width: 3 in / 7.6 cm

YARN
The Woobles Easy Peasy Yarn
or any medium-weight #4 yarn
Tan: This Sand is Your Sand,
40 yds / 36 m
Red: Let's Ketchup Soon,
30 yds / 27 m
White: Snow Place Like Home,
10 yds / 9 m
Brown: A Whole Latte Love,
2 yds / 2 m
Yellow: What's Up Buttercup,
1 yd / 1 m

CROCHET HOOK
US G-6 / 4mm

OTHER MATERIALS
 Stuffing
 Stitch marker
 Tapestry needle

VIDEOS
 thewoobles.com/celebrate

UPPER BASE

With tan yarn.

Rnd 1.   start 8 hdc in magic loop (8)

TIP Hdc means half double crochet. See tutorial on page 34.

Rnd 2.   8 hdc inc (16)

TIP Hdc inc means to crochet 2 hdc in the same stitch.

Rnd 3.   [hdc, hdc inc] x 8 (24)
Rnd 4.   [hdc inc, 2 hdc] x 8 (32)
Rnd 5.   [3 hdc, hdc inc] x 8 (40)

Invisible fasten off leaving a tail. Thread a needle with the tail of the **lower base**. Use it to sew the edge of the lower base to the center of the "right side" of the upper base.

TIP There's a so-called "right" and "wrong" side of crochet. See picture on page 22.

TOP

With red yarn.

Rnd 1.   start 8 hdc in magic loop (8)
Rnd 2.   8 hdc inc (16)
Rnd 3.   [hdc, hdc inc] x 8 (24)
Rnd 4.   [hdc inc, 2 hdc] x 8 (32)
Rnd 5.   32 hdc (32)
Rnd 6.   [3 hdc, hdc inc] x 8 (40)

Invisible fasten off leaving a long tail. Thread a needle with the tail. Use it to whip stitch the top to the open edge of the upper base. Make sure the "right side" of the top is facing out. Before you close the top completely, stuff it very lightly.

TIP See whip stitch tutorial on page 68.

DOOR

With brown yarn.

TIP This is an oval. See tutorial on page 48.

Rnd 1.   ch 4 (4)
Rnd 2.   2 sc, then 3 sc in the last st. Rotate the piece to work on the other side of the foundation chain. Sc, inc, sl st into the first sc of round 2. (8)
Rnd 3.   inc, sc, inc, 3 sc in same st, inc, sc, inc, 3 sc in same st (16)

Invisible fasten off leaving a long tail. Thread a needle with the tail. Use it to sew the door onto the lower base, spanning rounds 4 to 8.

DOORKNOB

With yellow yarn.

Embroider a doorknob on the right side of the door:

Step 1.
Thread a needle with a forearm's length of yarn. Insert the needle in the lower base, close to the door, and pull it out between the last two rounds of the right side of the door. Leave a 6-inch tail.

Step 2.
Insert the needle one stitch to the right, under the top loops of the last round. Insert the needle through the door and the base, and pull it out where the needle originally went into the piece, so that both yarn tails are coming out of the same hole. Tie a knot with both tails and hide them in the base.

SMALL WHITE SPOT

With white yarn.

Rnd 1.   start 6 sc in magic loop (6)

Invisible fasten off leaving a long tail.

MEDIUM WHITE SPOTS

With white yarn (make two).

Rnd 1.   start 8 sc in magic loop (8)

Invisible fasten off leaving a long tail.

LARGE WHITE SPOTS

With white yarn (make two).

Rnd 1.   start 6 sc in magic loop (6)
Rnd 2.   6 inc (12)

Invisible fasten off leaving a long tail. Thread a needle with the tail. Use it to sew each white spot to the mushroom top. Space them out a little randomly.

FINAL SIZE

Height: 4.5 in / 11.4 cm
Width: 6 in / 15.2 cm

YARN

The Woobles Easy Peasy Yarn
or any medium-weight #4 yarn
Blue: Seas the Day, 50 yds / 46 m
White: Snow Place Like Home,
10 yds / 9 m
Black: The Coal Shebang, 1 yd / 1 m
Green: Leaf It to Us, 2 yds / 2 m
Pink: Eat, Pink & Be Merry,
2 yds / 2 m
Orange: Orange You Glad,
2 yds / 2 m
Yellow: What's Up Buttercup,
2 yds / 2 m

CROCHET HOOK

US G-6 / 4mm

OTHER MATERIALS

 One pair of 10mm black
safety eyes
 Stuffing
 Stitch marker
Tapestry needle

VIDEOS

 thewoobles.com/celebrate

WALLY THE KOALA
Spend Some Koala-ty Time with Wine

Take a much-needed paws with Wally in order to sip and savor what matters most. He'll welcome your nearest and dearest from atop any wine bottle, while his colorful eucalyptus charms will help everyone hang onto the right glass. In fact, he'll make guests feel so at home that they may never want to leaf.

HEAD AND BODY

With blue yarn.

> **TIP** Keep track of where you are by placing a stitch marker in the first stitch of the current round. See tutorial on page 24.

Rnd 1.	start 6 sc in magic loop (6)
Rnd 2.	6 inc (12)
Rnd 3.	[sc, inc] x 6 (18)
Rnd 4.	[inc, 2 sc] x 6 (24)
Rnd 5.	24 sc (24)
Rnd 6.	[5 sc, inc] x 4 (28)
Rnds 7-9.	28 sc (28)
Rnd 10.	[6 sc, inc] x 4 (32)
Rnds 11-13.	32 sc (32)
Rnd 14.	[2 sc, dec] x 8 (24)
Rnd 15.	24 sc (24)
Rnd 16.	[sc, dec] x 8 (16)
Rnd 17.	16 sc (16)

Attach the eyes between rounds 7 and 8, with a 6-stitch space between them. If this amigurumi is for a baby or pet, embroider the eyes instead (see tutorial on page 56). Stuff the piece, shaping it like an egg.

Rnd 18.	8 dec (8)

Fasten off leaving a long tail. Thread a needle with the tail. Use it to pull the yarn tail through the front loops of each stitch. Pull tight to close the remaining gap.

EARS

With blue yarn (make two).

Rnd 1.   start 6 sc in magic loop (6)
Rnd 2.   6 inc (12)
Rnd 3.   [sc, inc] x 6 (18)
Rnd 4.   18 sc (18)
Rnd 5.   [sc, dec] x 6 (12)

Invisible fasten off leaving a long tail. Flatten the ears. Thread a needle with the tail. Use it to sew the ears onto either side of the head, spanning rounds 4 to 7.

INNER EAR FUZZ

With white yarn (make one in each ear).

Embroider five lines inside the ear, working in a fan shape, going from left to right. The top of each line should be about one round away from the outer edge of the ear.

Step 1.
Thread a needle with an arm's length of yarn. Insert the needle in the body and pull it out in the lower center of one of the ears, where the ear meets the body. Leave a 6-inch tail.

Step 2.
To make the first of the five lines, insert the needle to the left and pull it down out where the ear meets the body.

Step 3.
Continue embroidering lines in a fan shape by repeating step 2 four more times.

Step 4.
When you embroider the last line of the first ear, instead of pulling the needle out the same point, pull the needle out where the other ear meets the body.

Step 5.
Repeat steps 2-3 to embroider the other ear.

Step 6.
After you embroider the last line, pull the needle out of the body from the same place it went into originally, so that both yarn tails are coming out of the same hole. Tie a knot with both tails and hide them in the body.

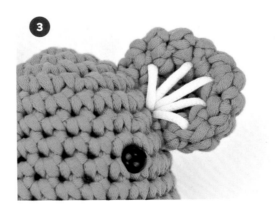

NOSE

With black yarn.

TIP This is an oval. See tutorial on page 48.

Rnd 1.   ch 4 (4)
Rnd 2.   2 sc, then 3 sc in the last st. Rotate the piece to work on the other side of the foundation chain. Sc, inc, sl st into the first sc of round 2. (8)

Invisible fasten off leaving a long tail. Thread a needle with the tail. Use it to sew the nose vertically onto the body spanning rounds 7 to 10, centered between the eyes.

BELLY

With white yarn.

Rnd 1.   start 6 sc in magic loop (6)
Rnd 2.   6 inc (12)
Rnd 3.   [sc, inc] x 6 (18)

Invisible fasten off leaving a long tail. Thread a needle with the tail. Use it to sew the belly onto the body centered below the nose, spanning rounds 12 to 16.

ARMS AND LEGS

With blue yarn (make four).

Rnd 1.   start 4 sc in magic loop (4)
Rnd 2.   [sc, inc] x 2 (6)
Rnds 3–8. 6 sc (6)

Invisible fasten off leaving a long tail. Thread a needle with the tail. Use it to sew all four arms and legs onto one side of the koala (left or right), so it can "hug" the neck of a bottle of wine. The arms should span rounds 9 and 10, and the legs should span rounds 15 and 16, with a 4-stitch space between each pair.

Thread the needle with an arm's length of yarn. Use it to sew the inside of the paws together:

Step 1.
Insert the needle through the outside of the back arm to the inside of the arm, between rounds 1 and 2. Leave a 6-inch tail.

Step 2.
Insert the needle in the equivalent spot on the inside of the front arm and pull it out one stitch down.

Step 3.
Insert the needle in the equivalent spot on the inside of the back arm and pull it out of the same hole that the yarn from step 1 is coming out of. Continue sewing, repeating steps 2-3, until the arms feel securely attached.

Step 4.
When you're done, pull the needle out of the piece through the same hole it originally went into, so that both yarn tails are coming out of the same hole. Do the same process with the koala's legs. Once the arms and legs are both secured, tie knots with their respective yarn tails and hide them in the piece.

LEAF

With green, pink, orange, and yellow yarn (make one in each color).

> **TIP** This is an oval, but with different stitches to make a leaf shape. See the oval tutorial on page 48.

Rnd 1. ch 7 (7)

Rnd 2. sc in the second st from the hook, hdc, 2 dc, hdc, inc. Rotate the piece to work on the other side of the foundation chain. Hdc, 2 dc, hdc, sc, sl st into the first sc of round 2. (12)

> **TIP** Hdc means half double crochet. See tutorial on page 34. Dc means double crochet. See tutorial on page 35.

Rnd 3. ch 18, sl st into the back loop of the eighth ch from hook (18)

> **TIP** blo means to do the stitch through the back loop only. See page 23 for a picture of a back loop.

Fasten off and weave the tail into the chain. To hang a leaf on a wine glass, wrap the chain around the wine glass stem and pull the leaf through the loop.

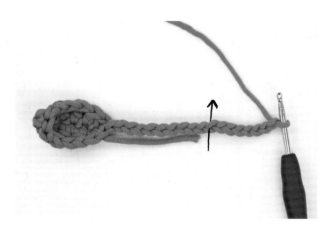

FINAL SIZE

Height: 3.5 in / 8.9 cm
Width: 4 in / 10.2 cm

YARN

The Woobles Easy Peasy Yarn
or any medium-weight #4 yarn
Pink: Eat, Pink & Be Merry,
50 yds / 46 m
Black: The Coal Shebang,
1 yd / 1 m

CROCHET HOOK

US G-6 / 4mm

OTHER MATERIALS

 One pair of 10mm black
safety eyes
 Potpourri
 Bag for potpourri
 Stitch marker
 Tapestry needle

VIDEOS

thewoobles.com/celebrate

PIPPA THE OCTOPUS

Keep Your New Home Smelling Ex-squid-site

With Pippa the Octopus, you'll be well-armed (eight of 'em!) against stale air and boring shelves. Whether manning a bathroom, closet, or coffee table, she's truly tentacular at keeping things fresh—while looking amaz-ink-ly debonair. So wherever she ends up, you'll be in for a kraken good time!

ARMS

With pink yarn (make eight).

TIP Keep track of where you are by placing a stitch marker in the first stitch of the current round. See page 24 for a tutorial.

Rnd 1.   start 6 sc in magic loop (6)
Rnds 2-5.   6 sc (6)

Stuff each arm lightly, and invisible fasten off leaving a tail.

HEAD AND BODY

With pink yarn.

▶ Video tutorial at **thewoobles.com/celebrate**

Rnd 1. Instead of sewing the arms onto the body, the body onto them:

Step 1.
Sl st join to a pair of opposite stitches of an arm.

> **TIP** Sl st join means slip stitch join. See tutorial on page 69.

Step 2.
Sc in the same spot as the sl st join. Sc through each remaining opposite pair of each arm. (24)

> **TIP** To secure the arm yarn tails, crochet over them like you would crochet over a different color yarn (see tutorial on page 50).

Rnd 2.	[2 sc, inc] x 8 (32)
Rnd 3.	32 sc (32)
Rnd 4.	[inc, 7 sc] x 4 (36)
Rnds 5–7.	36 sc (36)
Rnd 8.	[dec, 4 sc] x 6 (30)
Rnd 9.	30 sc (30)
Rnd 10.	[3 sc, dec] x 6 (24)
Rnd 11.	[dec, 2 sc] x 6 (18)
Rnd 12.	[sc, dec] x 6 (12)
Rnd 13.	6 dec (6)

Attach the eyes between rounds 6 and 7, with a 7-stitch space between them. If this amigurumi is for a baby or pet, embroider the eyes instead (see tutorial on page 56).

> **TIP** Remember that we made the octopus upside-down, so if you're counting rounds starting from the top of the head, the eyes look like they're between rounds 8 and 9 instead.

Thread a needle with the tail. Use it to pull the yarn tail through the front loops of each stitch. Pull tight to close the remaining gap.

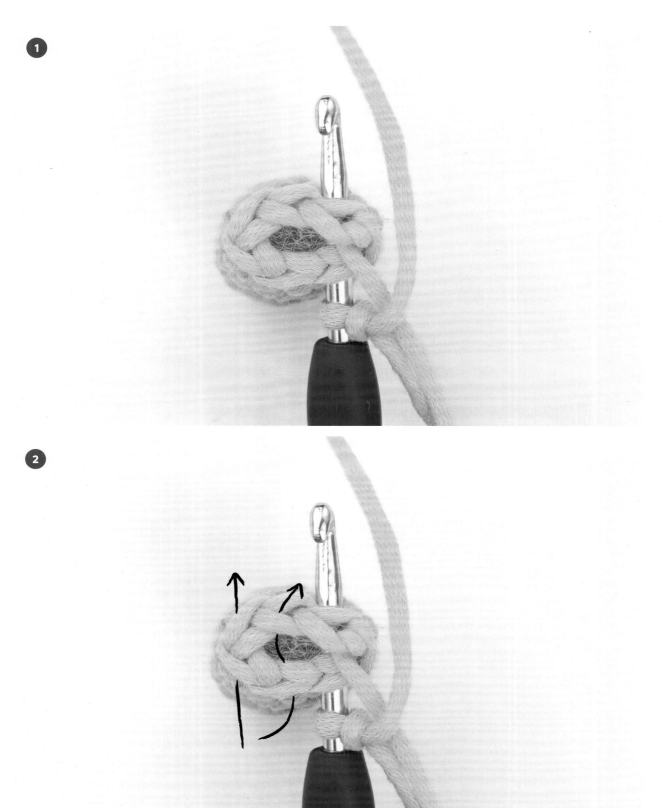

SMILE

With black yarn.

Since this piece won't be stuffed the usual way, embroider a curved smile now:

Step 1.
Thread a needle with a forearm's length of yarn. Insert the needle where you want the right corner of the smile to be, from the inside to the outside of the body.

Step 2.
Insert the needle back into the piece three stitches to the left (this is the other end of the smile). Pull it out of the piece one round down and equidistant between the two ends of the smile. Pull the yarn just tight enough so that the curve of the smile looks how you like.

Step 3.
Make sure you pulled the needle and yarn out of the piece below the curve. Then bring the needle up and over the curve and insert it back into the same hole it just came out of. Pull tight to secure the curve of the smile.

Step 4.
Both yarn tails should be on the inside of the piece. Double knot them as close to the piece as possible, and trim them short.

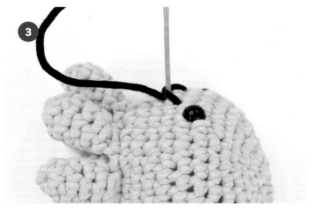

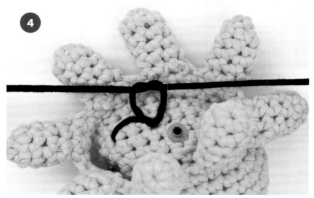

DRAWSTRING CLOSURE

With pink yarn.

Weave a drawstring closure so you can put in potpourri:

Step 1.
Thread a needle with an arm's length of yarn. Working on the inside of the octopus, insert the needle around one stitch in the middle of one arm in the round where the arm meets the body. Leave a 6-inch tail.

Step 2.
Insert the needle around one stitch in the middle of the next arm to the left, in the round where that arm meets the body. Repeat this step, working counterclockwise, until you've gone completely around the octopus.

Step 3.
Insert the bag of potpourri inside the octopus. Cut the yarn tails to equal lengths and pull on both tails to close the bottom opening of the octopus. Make a bow and hide the tails inside the octopus.

FINAL SIZE
Height: 6 in / 15.2 cm
Width: 2 in / 5.1 cm

YARN
The Woobles Easy Peasy Yarn
or any medium-weight #4 yarn
Green: Leaf It to Us, 40 yds / 36 m
Yellow: What's Up Buttercup,
9 yds / 8 m
Pink: Eat, Pink & Be Merry,
7 yd / 6 m
Blue: Seas the Day, 3 yds / 3 m

CROCHET HOOK
US G-6 / 4mm

OTHER MATERIALS
- ◉◉ One pair of 10mm black safety eyes
- ☁ Stuffing
- ◷ Stitch marker
- ✎ Tapestry needle
- 🍴 Dinner fork

VIDEOS
▶ thewoobles.com/celebrate

FRED THE DINO
Party Like It's 1999 B.C.

While it may look like Fred the Dino has a big bite, don't worry—he's mostly armless. With this pattern, you'll soon be dino-mite at crocheting anything round. Why? Because you'll be making lots of magic loops as you bring this adorably prehistoric Wooble to life. Once you master the magic loop with Fred the Dino, you'll be partying it up like it's 1999 B.C.

HEAD AND BODY

With green yarn.

TIP Keep track of where you are by placing a stitch marker in the first stitch of the current round. See tutorial on page 24.

Rnd 1.	start 6 sc in magic loop (6)
Rnd 2.	6 inc (12)
Rnd 3.	[sc, inc] x 6 (18)
Rnd 4.	[inc, 2 sc] x 6 (24)
Rnd 5.	6 sc, 8 inc, 10 sc (32)
Rnd 6.	[7 sc, inc] x 4 (36)
Rnds 7-8.	36 sc (36)
Rnd 9.	6 sc, [2 sc, dec] x 6, 6 sc (30)
Rnd 10.	6 sc, [dec, sc] x 6, 6 sc (24)
Rnd 11.	6 sc, 6 dec, 6 sc (18)
Rnd 12.	[2 sc, inc] x 6 (24)
Rnd 13.	24 sc (24)

Attach the eyes to the front side of the head (the side that sticks out more from the body) between rounds 6 and 7, with a 17-stitch space between them. If this amigurumi is for a baby or pet, embroider the eyes instead (see tutorial on page 56). Stuff the head.

Rnd 14.	[inc, 2 sc] x 8 (32)
Rnd 15.	32 sc (32)
Rnd 16.	[2 sc, dec] x 8 (24)
Rnd 17.	24 sc (24)
Rnd 18.	[dec, sc] x 8 (16)
Rnd 19.	16 sc (16)

Stuff the body.

Rnd 20.   8 dec (8)

Fasten off leaving a long tail. Thread a needle with the tail. Use it to pull the yarn tail through the front loops of each stitch. Pull tight to close the remaining gap.

TAIL

With green yarn.

Rnd 1.   start 4 sc in magic loop (4)
Rnd 2.   [sc, inc] x 2 (6)
Rnd 3.   2 sc, 2 inc, 2 sc (8)
Rnd 4.   3 sc, 2 inc, 3 sc (10)
Rnd 5.   4 sc, 2 inc, 4 sc (12)
Rnd 6.   5 sc, 2 inc, 5 sc (14)

Invisible fasten off leaving a long yarn tail. Stuff lightly. Thread a needle with the yarn tail. Use it to sew the dinosaur's tail piece to the middle of the dinosaur's back, spanning rounds 14 to 17. Make sure that the inclined part of the dinosaur tail, which is the side opposite the yarn tail, is facing up.

ARMS

With green yarn (make two).

▶ Video tutorial at **thewoobles.com/celebrate**

Repeat the following steps on each side to create two arms:

Step 1.
Sl st join the yarn to one side of the body between rounds 12 and 13, aligned roughly with the eyes. Insert the hook into the dinosaur's body from the back to the front of the body.

TIP Sl st join means slip stitch join. See tutorial on page 69.

Step 2.
Ch 3.

TIP When crocheting into a chain, crochet the first sc in the second chain from the hook.

Step 3.
2 sc.

Step 4.
Sl st in the stitch where you made the sl st join, from the front to the back of the body. Both yarn tails should be coming out of the same hole.

Step 5.
Fasten off. Tie the yarn tails together and hide them.

SPIKES

With yellow yarn (make five).

Rnd 1.   start 4 sc in magic loop (4)
Rnd 2.   [sc, inc] x 2 (6)

Invisible fasten off leaving a long yarn tail. Thread a needle with the yarn tail. Use it to sew the spike along the middle of the dinosaur's tail and back. Sew the first spike on at the tip of the dinosaur's tail and work your way up the back of the body, with 1 to 2 rounds spacing between each spike.

BELLY

With yellow yarn.

Thread a needle with an arm's length of yarn. Use it to embroider five belly stripes in horizontal lines, starting between the arms and working down the body:

Step 1.

Make the first belly stripe in between the arms. Insert the needle somewhere off to the side of the dinosaur and bring it out one stitch to the left of the right arm. Leave a 6-inch tail.

Step 2.

Insert the needle one stitch to the right of the left arm. Make the second stripe a little wider by bringing the needle out one round down and a little to the left.

Step 3.

Insert the needle in the same round but one stitch to the right of the right edge of the first stripe. Bring it out one round below and a little to the right.

Step 4.

Make a total of five stripes with this method. The fourth and fifth stripes should gradually get narrower.

Step 5.

When the last stripe is finished, bring the needle out where it originally started. Tie a knot with both yarn tails and hide them.

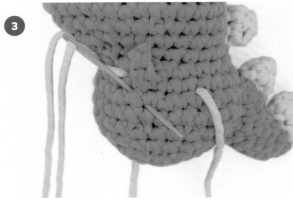

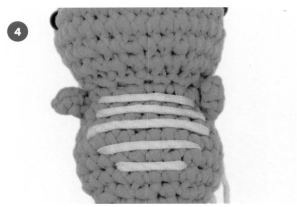

PARTY HAT

With pink and blue yarn.

Rnd 1.   (pink yarn) start 4 sc in magic loop (4)
Rnd 2.   4 inc (8)
Rnd 3.   8 sc (8)
Rnd 4.   [sc, inc] x 4 (12)
Rnd 5.   12 sc (12)

> **TIP** You're changing colors in the next round. Remember to switch colors in the last step of the stitch before the color change. See tutorial on page 50.

Rnd 6.   (switch to blue yarn) [inc, 2 sc] x 4 (16)

Invisible fasten off the blue yarn, and weave in the tail. Leave a long tail of pink yarn. You'll use this to make a strap for the party hat:

Step 1.
Thread a needle with the pink yarn tail. Use it to string the party hat securely around the dinosaur's chin. Insert the needle under the top loops of the blue round, from the bottom up.

Step 2.
Then insert the needle under the same spot again, from the bottom up, to make a loop.

Step 3.
Pull the needle through the loop made in step 2; then pull tight. Finally, weave in the yarn tail.

POM-POM

With blue yarn.

Cut an arm's length of blue yarn and set it aside. You'll use this later to hold the pom-pom together and sew it to the hat. With the rest of the yarn and a fork (prongs pointing to the right), make the body of the pom-pom:

Step 1.
Hold the yarn tail at the bottom left-hand corner of the fork; then wrap it over the second prong of the fork.

Step 2.
Wrap the yarn under the third prong and over the first prong.

Step 3.
Wrap the yarn around the top and bottom prongs of the fork 15 times. Then cut the yarn.

Step 4.
Take the arm's length of yarn you set aside earlier and double knot it very tightly around the middle of the yarn wrapped around the fork.

Step 5.
Slide the yarn off of the fork and cut open the loops.

Step 6.
Trim the yarn until it looks like a fluffy sphere. Make sure you don't cut the yarn tails from the arm's length of yarn that's holding the middle of the pom-pom together!

Step 7.
Take the party hat off of the dinosaur if you haven't already done so. Place the pom-pom at the top of the hat. Using a hook or needle, carefully pull one yarn tail through the center tip of the hat, and pull the other yarn tail through a hole one stitch away.

Step 8.
At this point, both yarn tails should be on the inside of the hat. Double knot the two tails as close as possible to the hat. Cut the tails so that there's still some tail left, but short enough that the hat hides them.

TIP Flip the hat inside out to make sure you knot the yarn tails as close to the hat as possible.

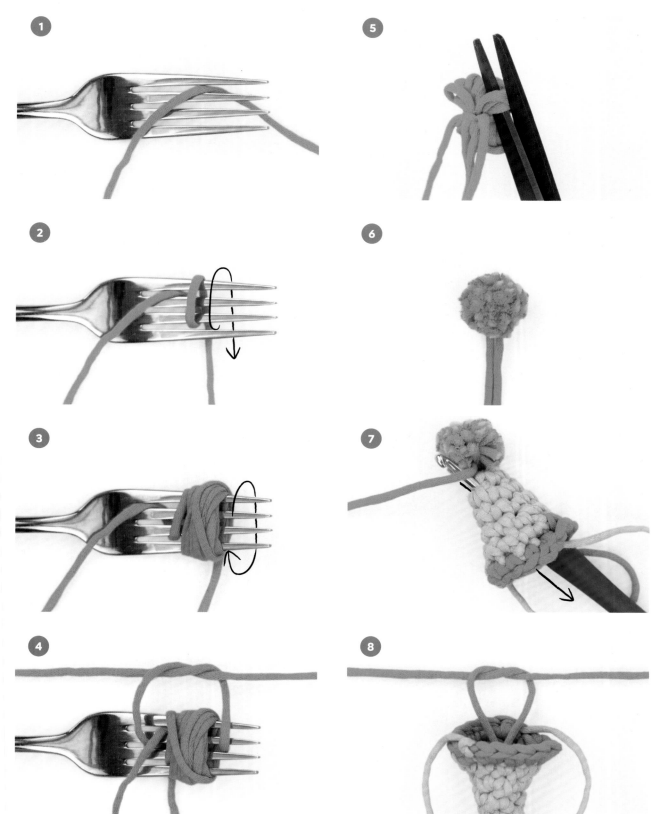

FINAL SIZE

Height: 3.5 in / 8.9 cm
Width: 4 in / 10.2 cm

YARN

The Woobles Easy Peasy Yarn
or any medium-weight #4 yarn
Brown: A Whole Latte Love,
50 yds / 46 m
Tan: This Sand is Your Sand,
7 yds / 6 m
Dark brown: Chocolate Moose,
3 yds / 3 m
Blue: Seas the Day, 5 yds / 5 m
Yellow: What's Up Buttercup,
5 yds / 5 m
Pink: Eat, Pink & Be Merry,
5 yds / 5 m

CROCHET HOOK

US G-6 / 4mm

OTHER MATERIALS

- ◎◎ One pair of 10mm black
  safety eyes
- Stuffing
- Stitch marker
- Tapestry needle
- Three toothpicks

VIDEOS

▷ thewoobles.com/celebrate

SAM THE SLOTH
Wishing You a Sloth-a Fun

Have someone you enjoy hangin' with? Give them Sam the Sloth to remind them it's totally OK to laze about, take things slow, and enjoy each and every day–not just their special day. Hope you don't mind we got a little philo-sloth-ical there.

HEAD AND BODY

With brown yarn.

TIP Keep track of where you are by placing a stitch marker in the first stitch of the current round. See tutorial on page 24.

Rnd 1.	start 6 sc in magic loop (6)
Rnd 2.	6 inc (12)
Rnd 3.	[sc, inc] x 6 (18)
Rnd 4.	[inc, 2 sc] x 6 (24)
Rnd 5.	24 sc (24)
Rnd 6.	[5 sc, inc] x 4 (28)
Rnds 7-9.	28 sc (28)
Rnd 10.	[6 sc, inc] x 4 (32)
Rnds 11-13.	32 sc (32)
Rnd 14.	[2 sc, dec] x 8 (24)
Rnd 15.	24 sc (24)
Rnd 16.	[sc, dec] x 8 (16)
Rnd 17.	16 sc (16)

Stuff the piece.

Rnd 18.	8 dec (8)

Fasten off leaving a long tail. Thread a needle with the tail. Use it to pull the yarn tail through the front loops of each stitch. Pull tight to close the remaining gap.

FACE

With tan yarn.

TIP This is an oval. See tutorial on page 48.

Rnd 1.   ch 6 (6)
Rnd 2.   4 sc, then 3 sc in the last stitch. Rotate the piece to work on the other side of the foundation chain. 3 sc, inc, sl st into the first sc of round 2 (12)
Rnd 3.   [3 sc, 3 inc] x 2 (18)
Rnd 4.   3 sc, [sc, inc] x 3, 3 sc, [sc, inc] x 3 (24)

Invisible fasten off leaving a long tail. Thread a needle with the tail. Use it to sew the face onto the body, spanning rounds 5 to 10.

EYES, NOSE, AND MOUTH

With dark brown yarn (make two).

TIP This is an oval. See tutorial on page 48.

Rnd 1.   ch 4 (4)
Rnd 2.   2 sc, then 3 sc in the last stitch. Rotate the piece to work on the other side of the foundation chain. Sc, inc, sl st into the first sc of round 2 (8)

Invisible fasten off leaving a long tail. Now sew the eye pieces to the sloth and embroider a nose and mouth:

Step 1.

Attach a safety eye one round in from the short edge of each dark brown eye piece, in between rounds 1 and 2. If this amigurumi is for a baby or pet, embroider the eye instead (see tutorial on page 56).

Step 2.

Line up the dark brown eye pieces on either side of the tan face piece, so that the eyes are two rounds in from the short edge of the tan piece. Make sure to position the eye pieces pointing down at a 45-degree angle to create that signature droopy-eyed sloth look.

Step 3.

Thread a needle with the yarn tail of the eye piece. Use it to sew the eye pieces to the sloth.

Step 4.

Thread a needle with an arm's length of dark brown yarn. Use it to embroider a nose and mouth (see tutorial on page 60). The nose should be in the middle of the tan face. The bottom of the line should be two rounds below the nose.

ARMS AND LEGS

With brown and tan yarn (make four).

Rnd 1. (brown yarn) start 4 sc in magic loop (4)
Rnd 2. [sc, inc] x 2 (6)
Rnds 3–6. 6 sc (6)

Invisible fasten off leaving a long tail. Thread a needle with the yarn tail. Use it to sew the arms and legs onto one side of the sloth (left or right). The arms should span rounds 10 and 11, and the legs should span rounds 14 and 15. There should be a 4-stitch space between the arms and a 3-stitch space between the legs.

Thread a needle with an arm's length of tan yarn. Use it to sew the paws together to create the look of claws so the sloth can "hold" the balloons. Do these steps twice–once for the arms, once for legs:

▶ Video tutorial at **thewoobles.com/celebrate**

Step 1.
Insert the needle through the sloth's back paw from the inside to the outside of the paw, one round down from the tip of the paw. Leave a 6-inch tail.

Step 2.
Pull the needle through the equivalent spot on the front paw, but this time, bring the needle from the outside to the inside of the arm.

Step 3.
Insert the needle back into the same spot it just came out of, but only through the inside layer of the paw–then pull it out of the front side of the same paw, one stitch down.

Step 4.
Make sure the tan yarn wraps around the outside of the paws. Pull the needle through the equivalent spot on the back paw, from the outside in, so that both yarn tails are coming out of the same hole.

Step 5.
Pull tight so that the tan yarn wraps around the outside of the paws, like claws. Tie a knot with both yarn tails and hide them.

BALLOONS

With blue, pink, and yellow yarn (make three, one in each color).

Rnd 1.   start 6 sc in magic loop (6)
Rnd 2.   6 inc (12)
Rnds 3–4.   12 sc (12)
Rnd 5.   [sc, dec] x 4 (8)

Stuff lightly.

TIP Since the balloon is so small, it can be easier to work with if you stuff it with scrap pieces of yarn instead of stuffing.

Rnd 6.   4 dec (4)
Rnd 7.   4 sl st flo (4)

TIP flo means to do the stitch through the front loop only. See page 23 for a picture of a front loop.

Invisible fasten off. Pull the yarn tail through the center bottom of the balloon to help round out the shape. Push each balloon onto the pointy side of a toothpick. Push the toothpicks with the balloons through the arms and legs.

FINAL SIZE

Height: 6.5 in / 16.5 cm
Width: 5 in / 12.7 cm

YARN

The Woobles Easy Peasy Yarn
or any medium-weight #4 yarn
Tan: This Sand is Your Sand,
40 yds / 36 m
Dark brown: Chocolate Moose,
16 yds / 15 m
Blue: Seas the Day, 8 yds / 7 m
White: Snow Place Like Home,
12 yds / 11 m
Yellow: What's Up Buttercup,
1 yd / 1 m
Black: The Coal Shebang, 1 yd / 1 m
Orange: Orange You Glad,
0.5 yds / 0.5 m

CROCHET HOOK

US G-6 / 4mm

OTHER MATERIALS

 One pair of 10mm black
safety eyes
 Stuffing
 Stitch marker
 Tapestry needle

VIDEOS

 thewoobles.com/celebrate

DOUG THE PUG
It's Paw-ty Time

Doug the Pug loves being the life of the paw-ty. After all, what's the best way to celebrate someone? With lots of pugs and kisses. Some might think his hat is a bit over the top, but he's all about being that round pug in a square hole. Make him once, and you'll wonder howl you ever had a paw-ty without him.

HEAD AND BODY

With tan yarn.

TIP Keep track of where you are by placing a stitch marker in the first stitch of the current round. See page 24 for a tutorial.

Rnd 1.	start 6 sc in magic loop (6)
Rnd 2.	6 inc (12)
Rnd 3.	[sc, inc] x 6 (18)
Rnd 4.	[inc, 2 sc] x 6 (24)
Rnd 5.	24 sc (24)
Rnd 6.	[5 sc, inc] x 4 (28)
Rnds 7-9.	28 sc (28)
Rnd 10.	[6 sc, inc] x 4 (32)
Rnds 11-13.	32 sc (32)
Rnd 14.	[2 sc, dec] x 8 (24)
Rnd 15.	24 sc (24)
Rnd 16.	[sc, dec] x 8 (16)
Rnd 17.	16 sc (16)

Attach the eyes between rounds 7 and 8 with a 6-stitch space between them. If this amigurumi is for a baby or pet, embroider the eyes instead (see tutorial on page 56). Stuff the piece.

Rnd 18.   8 dec (8)

Fasten off leaving a long tail. Thread a needle with the tail. Use it to pull the yarn tail through the front loops of each stitch. Pull tight to close the remaining gap.

SNOUT

With dark brown and black yarn.

TIP This is an oval , but with different stitches to create a V shape. See tutorial on page 48.

Rnd 1. (dark brown yarn) ch 8 (8)

Rnd 2. 3 sc, [3 sc in the same stitch], 2 sc, [3 sc in the last st]. Rotate the piece to work on the other side of the foundation chain. 5 sc, inc in the very first ch. Sl st in the first sc of round 2. (18)

Invisible fasten off leaving a long tail. The snout should look like a V. Sew it so the V looks like it's upside-down, in the middle of the eyes, spanning rounds 8 to 11.

Thread a needle with an arm's length of black yarn. Use it to embroider a nose and mouth (see tutorial on page 60). The nose should be one round down from the top edge of the snout. The bottom of the vertical line should be at the bottom of the snout.

EARS

With dark brown yarn (make two).

Rnd 1. start 6 sc in magic loop (6)

Rnd 2. 6 inc (12)

Rnds 3-4. 12 sc (12)

Rnd 5. [sc, dec] x 4 (8)

Rnd 6. 8 sc (8)

Invisible fasten off leaving a long tail. Flatten the ear and whip stitch the two sides together. Sew the ears on the sides of the pug in between rounds 4 and 5.

TIP See whip stitch tutorial on page 68.

CAKE HAT

With white and blue yarn.

Rnd 1.   (white yarn) start 6 sc in magic loop (6)

Rnd 2.   6 inc (12)

Rnd 3.   [sc, inc] x 6 (18)

> **TIP** You're changing colors in the next round. Remember to switch colors in the last step of the stitch before the color change. See tutorial on page 50.

Rnd 4.   (switch to blue yarn) 18 sc blo (18)

> **TIP** blo means to do the stitch through the back loop only. See page 23 for a picture of a back loop.

Rnds 5–9.   18 sc (18)

Rnd 10.   (switch to white yarn) [sl st, ch 2, dc4tog] x 9 (36)

> **TIP** Dc4tog means double crochet 4 stitches together. It's similar to a dc5tog, but with one less dc. See dc5tog tutorial on page 36.

Sl st into the first sl st of round 10. The bottom edge of the hat (the bottom frosting trim) should flare out.

Fasten off leaving a long tail. You'll use this tail to sew the hat to the pug after making the top frosting trim and flame.

Next, make the frosting trim on the top of the hat:

Step 1.
Sl st join the white yarn through one of the front loops from round 4, then dc in same stitch.

> **TIP** Dc means double crochet. See tutorial on page 35.

Step 2.
In each front loop of round 4, sl st and dc in same stitch.

Step 3.
Sl st in the front loop where you did the sl st join in step 1. Fasten off and weave in the yarn tail.

FLAME

With yellow and orange yarn.

> **TIP** This is an oval, but with different stitches to make a flame shape. See the oval tutorial on page 48.

Rnd 1. (yellow yarn) ch 5 (5)

Rnd 2. Sl st, hdc, sc, sl st, ch 1. Rotate the piece to work on the other side of the foundation chain. Sl st, sc, hdc, sl st. Sl st into the first stitch of round 2. (9)

Fasten off leaving a long tail. Thread a needle with the tail. Use it to sew the flame to the center top of the hat.

Make the inner flame detail:

Step 1.
Thread a needle with a forearm's length of orange yarn. Insert the needle up from inside the hat and out the top immediately next to the flame, leaving a 6-inch tail.

Step 2.
Pull the needle through the middle of the flame and insert it back down through the top of the hat on the other side of the flame to secure it to the hat.

Step 3.
Both yarn tails should be on the inside of the hat. Double knot the two tails together as close as possible to the hat. Cut the tails so that there's still some tail left, but short enough that the hat hides them.

> **TIP** Flip the hat inside out to make sure you knot the yarn tails as close to the hat as possible.

Thread a needle with the white tail of the hat. Use it to sew the hat to the top of the pug.

FINAL SIZE
Height: 4 in / 10.2 cm
Width: 3 in / 7.6 cm

YARN

The Woobles Easy Peasy Yarn
or any medium-weight #4 yarn

Brown: A Whole Latte Love,
40 yds / 36 m

Tan: This Sand is Your Sand,
6 yds / 5 m

White: Snow Place Like Home,
7 yds / 6 m

Yellow: What's Up Buttercup,
50 yds / 46 m

Red: Let's Ketchup Soon, 2 yds / 2 m

Green: Leaf It to Us, 1 yd / 1 m

Blue: Seas the Day, 1 yd / 1 m

Orange: Orange You Glad, 1 yd / 1 m

Black: The Coal Shebang, 1 yd / 1 m

CROCHET HOOK

US G-6 / 4mm

OTHER MATERIALS

- One pair of 10mm black safety eyes
- Stuffing
- Stitch marker
- Tapestry needle

VIDEOS

 thewoobles.com/celebrate

WALTER THE BEAR
A Bear-y Happy Birthday

Is it a bear? A cupcake? Or a bear-cake? We're not sure, and that's OK. In fact, we daresay that's what gives Walter the Bear his un-bear-able charm. Wondering if this pattern is a little outside the realm of paws-ibility for a beginner? Don't sweat it—he may have more parts than your average Wooble, but he's only made with basic stitches. We promise it'll totally be worth it when you get to show off what you've made with your bear hands.

HEAD AND BODY

With brown yarn.

> **TIP** Keep track of where you are by placing a stitch marker in the first stitch of the current round. See tutorial on page 24.

Rnd 1.	start 6 sc in magic loop (6)
Rnd 2.	6 inc (12)
Rnd 3.	[sc, inc] x 6 (18)
Rnd 4.	[inc, 2 sc] x 6 (24)
Rnd 5.	24 sc (24)
Rnd 6.	[5 sc, inc] x 4 (28)
Rnds 7-9.	28 sc (28)
Rnd 10.	[6 sc, inc] x 4 (32)
Rnds 11-13.	32 sc (32)
Rnd 14.	[2 sc, dec] x 8 (24)
Rnd 15.	24 sc (24)
Rnd 16.	[sc, dec] x 8 (16)
Rnd 17.	16 sc (16)

Attach the eyes between rounds 7 and 8 with a 6-stitch space between them. If this amigurumi is for a baby or pet, embroider the eyes instead (see tutorial on page 56). Stuff the piece, shaping it like an egg.

Rnd 18.	8 dec (8)

Fasten off leaving a long tail. Thread a needle with the tail and pull it through the front loops of each stitch. Pull tight to close the remaining gap.

SNOUT

With tan and black yarn.

TIP This is an oval. See tutorial on page 48.

Rnd 1.   (tan yarn) ch 4 (4)
Rnd 2.   2 sc, then 3 sc in the last st. Rotate the piece to work on the other side of the foundation chain. Sc, inc, sl st into the first sc of round 2. (8)
Rnd 3.   [2 sc, 2 inc] x 2 (12)
Rnd 4.   12 sc (12)

Invisible fasten off, leaving a long tail. Stuff lightly. Thread a needle with the tail. Use it to sew the snout between the eyes, spanning rounds 7 to 10.

TIP Since the snout is so small, it can be easier to work with if you stuff it with scrap pieces of yarn instead of stuffing.

To make the nose and mouth, thread the needle with an arm's length of black yarn. Embroider a nose and mouth (see tutorial on page 60). The nose should be one round higher than the middle of the snout. The bottom of the vertical line should be one round below the nose.

EARS

With brown yarn (make two).

Rnd 1.   start 4 sc in magic loop (4)
Rnd 2.   4 inc (8)
Rnd 3.   8 sc (8)

Invisible fasten off, leaving a long tail. Thread a needle with the tail. Use it to sew the right ear onto the body, spanning rounds 4 to 6. Don't sew the other ear on yet.

FROSTING

With white yarn.

▶ Video tutorial at **thewoobles.com/celebrate**

Rnd 1.   start 6 sc in magic loop (6)
Rnd 2.   6 inc (12)
Rnd 3.   [sc, inc] x 6 (18)
Rnd 4.   This round is worked in steps into round 3 to make the drips of the frosting:

Step 1.

Sc, sl st, ch 3, 2 sc.

TIP When crocheting into a chain, crochet the first sc in the second chain from the hook.

Step 2.

Sc, sl st, ch 4, 3 sc.

Step 3.

Repeat steps 1-2 three times.

Step 4.

Sc, sl st, ch 2, sc, sl st in the first stitch from step 1.

Fasten off leaving a long tail. Thread a needle with the tail. Use it to sew the frosting onto the top of the bear's head, a little off to the left (make sure not to cover the eye). Sew the left ear on top of the frosting, using the right ear as a reference point.

CHERRY

With red yarn.

Rnd 1.	start 4 sc in magic loop (4)
Rnd 2.	4 inc (8)
Rnd 3.	8 sc (8)
Rnd 4.	4 dec (4)

Fasten off leaving a long tail. Thread a needle with the tail. Use it to pull the yarn tail through the front loops of each stitch. Pull tight to close the remaining gap. Then pull the needle through the middle of the last round and out the other side. Leave the tail. You'll use it to sew the cherry onto the bear later.

CHERRY STEM

With green yarn.

Row 1.	ch 4 (4)

> **TIP** When crocheting a new row, remember to skip the first stitch from the hook. And for the first row after a chain, remember to crochet under the back loops only. See tutorial on page 47.

Row 2.	3 sl st (3)

Fasten off leaving a long tail. Thread a needle with the tail. Use it to sew the stem to the cherry:

Step 1.
Insert the needle in and out of the top of the cherry, around one stitch and opposite the red yarn tail. Pull tight.

Step 2.
Insert the needle through the bottom of the stem. Pull tight.

Step 3.
Insert the needle in and out of the same spots on top of the cherry.

Step 4.
Before pulling tight, put the needle through the loop made in step 3. Then hide the stem yarn tails.

Use the cherry yarn tail to sew the cherry to the bear's head on top of the frosting, a little closer to the left ear. The stem should face up and a little toward the back.

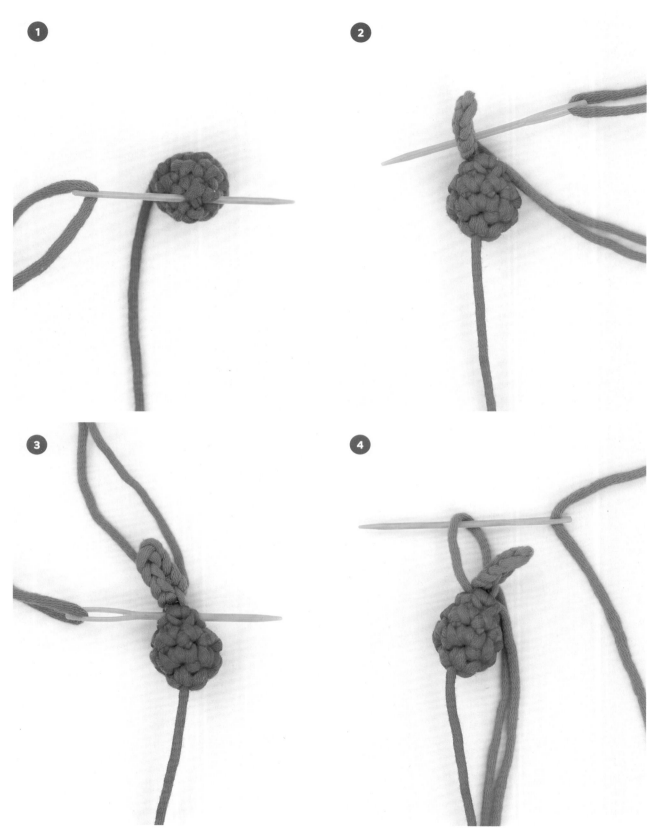

SPRINKLES

With blue, orange, and yellow yarn.

To embroider sprinkles, thread a needle with an arm's length of yarn. Insert the needle into and out of the frosting piece in random directions and with random spacing, spanning either one stitch or one round. After you embroider the last sprinkle in a color, pull the needle out of the piece from the same place it went into originally, so that both yarn tails are coming out of the same hole. Tie a knot with both tails and hide them in the body.

Repeat this with each color until you have a nice sprinkling of sprinkles.

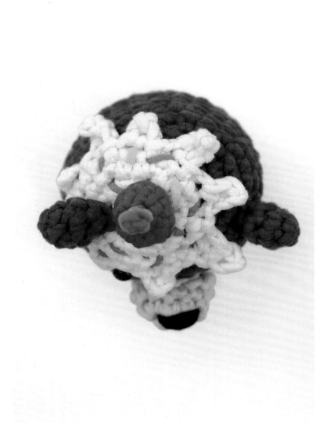

CUPCAKE LINER

With yellow yarn.

Row 1.   ch 8 (8)

TIP When crocheting a new row, remember to skip the first stitch from the hook. And for the first row after a chain, remember to crochet under the back loops only. See tutorial on page 47.

Rows 2–35. 7 sc blo, ch 1 and turn (7)

TIP blo means to do the stitch through the back loop only. See page 23 for a picture of a back loop.

Row 36.   7 sc blo, ch 1 (7)

Rotate the piece to work round 37 and the following rounds along the long edge of the piece.

▶ Video tutorial at **thewoobles.com/celebrate**

Rnd 37.   [3 sc, dec] x 7 (28)

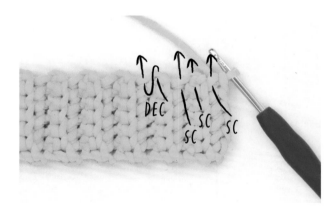

Rnd 38.   28 sc blo (28)

Rnd 39.   [2 sc, dec] x 7 (21)
Rnd 40.   [dec, sc] x 7 (14)
Rnd 41.   7 dec (7)

Fasten off leaving a long tail. Thread a needle with the tail. Use it to pull the yarn tail through the front loops of each stitch. Pull tight to close the remaining gap.

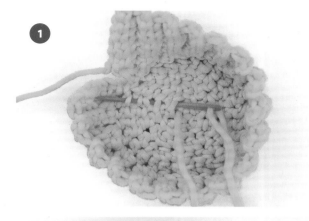

Now, use the same long yarn tail to sew the seam of the cupcake liner closed:

Step 1.
Weave the yarn tail through some stitches on the inside of the piece until you get to where the two open edges of the cupcake liner meet.

Step 2.
Whip stitch the seam closed.

TIP See whip stitch tutorial on page 68.

Step 3.
Then weave in the yarn tail.

Tuck the bear into his cupcake liner home (no sewing required)—and try to resist the temptation to gobble him up!

RESOURCES

THE WOOBLES EASY PEASY YARN

To make Woobles that look just like the ones in this book, use The Woobles Easy Peasy yarn. It can't fray and it can't snag, making it easy peasy to crochet with. Buy it on our website.

thewoobles.com/yarn

STITCH AND TECHNIQUE TUTORIALS

General video and photo crochet tutorials are available here.

thewoobles.com/tutorials

PATTERN TUTORIALS

Looking for video tutorials for specific patterns in this book? Look no further.

thewoobles.com/celebrate

THE WOOBLES CROCHET KITS

Want a more guided crochet experience? Snag a Woobles crochet kit.

thewoobles.com/kits

THE WOOBLES COMMUNITY

Get tips and tricks from other Wooblers, share your crochet creations, and spread good vibes all around.

thewoobles.com/community

ACKNOWLEDGMENTS

I want to thank:

Claire, for making this book a reality. For giving The Woobles a try when we were only a few months old and seeing potential in us. For convincing me to write this book even though it seemed like a big scary thing, and then convincing the Insight Editions team to publish it. For making the big scary book writing process such a smooth like butter experience, and for being someone who I can 100% rely on (which is extremely important because did I mention that writing a book is a big scary thing?).

BJ, for teaching this self-taught crocheter the ways of the trade. Thanks for being patient with me and making my patterns so much more on the mark. (Look ma, I'm a legit crochet designer now!)

Colleen, for always presenting The Woobles in the best light. Literally. Thank you for bringing The Woobles to life with the most abso-friggin' adorable photos, for keeping your cool as I ask you to nudge things a little to the left and a little to the right and then back to the left again, and for being that perfect mix of scrappy and professional. It's always tons of fun talking to you; I wish every meeting I had was filled with as much laughter and wonder as phone calls with you! I love your hustle, good vibes, and woobly spirit. Wooble on, my friend!

Everyone on the Insight Editions team, especially Lola and Chrissy, for doing all the work behind the scenes to turn this book from pixels on a screen into the beautiful pages sitting before you. Also huge shout out to Allie, who introduced Claire to The Woobles and then blew my mind with what I can only call "word magic." I thank you on behalf of all the Wooblers out there for making this book super duper crystal clear and consistent.

Sahngmie, for your otter-ly unbe-leaf-able a-bee-lity to sling pun after pun after pun. When we first star-ted working together, I wasn't pre-pear-ed to witness such toad-al word mastery. Your descriptions are always a whole sloth-a cute, clever, and fun. Thank ewe for being prickin' claw-some, and peas keep it coming!

Danka, for taking our brand to the next level. I've said it to you time and time again, and I feel the need to put it in here so it can be on the record forever. You're one of the best designers I've ever worked with. I'm so incredibly grateful for your eye, your honesty, and your amazing ability to come up with thoughtful solutions to any situation. Thanks for being a part of team Woobles.

My husband, Adrian, what're you doing reading this? Get back to work. Just kidding. Thanks for being the perfect other half of The Woobles. For keeping the business afloat whenever I went into my pattern designing hidey hole, for spending our 14-year anniversary (and the days before and after it) cutting, assembling, and folding paper for this book, and for always making work feel like play. I roverbots you, boo.

My parents and my in-laws, Connie, Romeo, Jane, and Jack, for being a major force behind getting The Woobles off the ground. Thanks for being with us from day one, back when we spun yarn balls on Sharpies. For spending a ridiculous amount of time assembling crochet kits and shipping packages with us. And most of all, thanks for being chill about us quitting our stable careers, moving home, and taking over your basements to chase the dream.

My sister, Danica, for dubbing thee The Woobles. Your naming prowess is like no other.

All the Wooblers. All those nice things you emailed, DM'd, and wrote in Facebook comments? I read them all, and they made me feel like I did something good for the world. Thank you so much for supporting us, and for sticking around for the ride–The Woobles wouldn't be here without you.

On the flip side of that, The Woobles team. We're just a wee woobly company, but we've done amazing things together. Because of you, we've been able to drop these little nuggets of happiness and confidence-boosters all over the world. Thank you for woobling with us!

All our friends who agreed to be our guinea pigs, rah-rah-rahed for us, and had no interest in learning to crochet but bought a kit anyway. That's you: Adam, Alice, Amanda, Amy, Andy, Angelo, Audrey, Brigitte, Brittney, Carol, Charlie, Chris, Cinthya, Connie, D Lee, Dan, Daniel, David, Deborah, Dragan, Eric, Gabe, Garrett, Greg, Guolin, Hannah, Heidi, Jay, Jenny, Joy, K Tao, K Wang, Kathleen, Kelsey, Leo, Lisa, Liza, Marcy, Mathias, Matt, Nasia, Odell, Ope, Oreo, Pea, Rachael, Sabrina, Serena, Shannon, other Shannon, Sharon, Shawn, Shirley, Shuper, Simon, Souvik, Susan, Wang Lin, Wei, Yang, @curiouspapaya, @sweetyippiecrafts

ABOUT THE AUTHOR

Justine got her design chops at Google, where she led User Experience Design for Google Classroom and made new products like Google Expeditions. While it was great fun watching kids hold up pieces of cardboard to their faces and run into lockers (RIP Expeditions), she was more touched by how a well-designed learning experience transformed how people felt about themselves.

Justine started The Woobles because she realized we could all use the excitement and confidence boost that comes from learning something new.

Justine is always wooblin'. She also cooks, eats, sleeps, and takes the occasional trip. Sometimes she manages to fit in a workout here and there. One day she hopes to fill the dog-shaped void in her heart too.

Her favorite food is fried chicken (It's Bo Time). Her favorite animal is a dog (see void in her heart). Her favorite person is her husband (who also happens to be her favorite coworker).

ABOUT THE WOOBLES

The Woobles makes learn-to-crochet kits for complete beginners. Since 2020, wife-and-husband team Justine and Adrian have taught tens of thousands of beginners to crochet (and counting!)

Our kits work because they come with more than just the materials you need—we're talking things like step-by-step videos, no-fray Easy Peasy yarn custom-made for beginners, and a pre-started piece so you can jump right into learning the basics.

While we've put a lot of thought into how to give you a yarn good first crocheting experience, it's not actually about crochet. It's about proving to yourself that you can always learn something new. That you can take on whatever comes your way.

thewoobles.com – @thewoobles

weldon**owen**

An Imprint of Insight Editions
PO Box 3088
San Rafael, CA 94912
www.weldonowen.com

CEO Raoul Goff
VP Publisher Roger Shaw
Editorial Director Katie Killebrew
Editor Claire Yee
VP Creative Chrissy Kwasnik
Designer Lola Villanueva
VP Manufacturing Alix Nicholaeff
Production Manager Joshua Smith
Sr Production Manager, Subsidiary Rights Lina Palma-Temena

Weldon Owen would also like to thank Dyad Photography, Allie Kiekhofer,
 and Hilary Flood.

Text © 2022 Justine Tiu

Photography © 2022 Weldon Owen International

ISBN: 978-1-68188-856-9

Manufactured in China by Insight Editions

10 9 8 7 6

2026 2025 2024

ROOTS of PEACE   REPLANTED PAPER

Insight Editions, in association with Roots of Peace, will plant two trees for each tree used in
the manufacturing of this book. Roots of Peace is an internationally renowned humanitarian
organization dedicated to eradicating land mines worldwide and converting war-torn lands
into productive farms and wildlife habitats. Roots of Peace will plant two million fruit and nut
trees in Afghanistan and provide farmers there with the skills and support necessary for
sustainable land use.